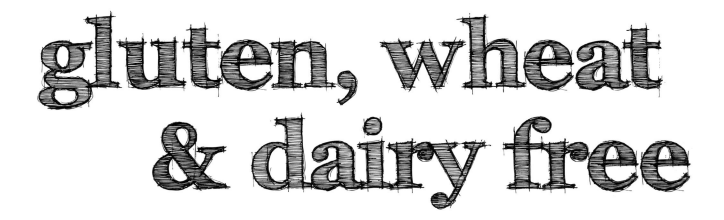

gluten, wheat & dairy free

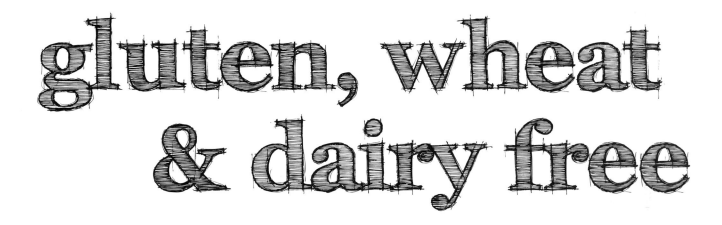

gluten, wheat & dairy free

LOVE FOOD™

This edition published in 2011
LOVE FOOD is an imprint of Parragon Books Ltd

Parragon
Queen Street House
4 Queen Street
Bath BA1 1HE, UK

ISBN: 978-1-4454-5883-0

Printed in China

Additional photography by Clive Streeter
Food styling by Teresa Goldfinch
Additional recipes and introduction written by Christine France

Notes for the Reader
This book uses standard kitchen measuring spoons and cups, and all spoon and cup measurements are level unless otherwise indicated. Unless otherwise stated, milk is assumed to be whole, eggs are large, individual fruit and vegetables are medium, and pepper is freshly ground black pepper.

The times given are only an approximate guide. Preparation times differ according to the techniques used by different people and the cooking times may also vary from those given. Optional ingredients, variations, or serving suggestions have not been included in the calculations.

Recipes using raw or very lightly cooked eggs should be avoided by infants, the elderly, pregnant women, convalescents, and anyone whose health is compromised by a chronic illness. Pregnant and breast-feeding women are advised to avoid eating peanuts and peanut products. People with nut allergies should be aware that some of the prepared ingredients used in the recipes in this book may contain nuts. Always check the packaging before use.

The publisher has been careful to select ingredients for the recipes used in this book that will not cause a problem for anyone who is sensitive to wheat, gluten, or dairy. However, always read labels carefully and, if necessary, check with the manufacturer.

The nutritional information is given per serving and does not include the "to serve" suggestions. Readers are advised that the salt amounts shown per recipe do not take into account any salt which may be added to taste, or at the table. Any ingredients that do not contain a weight measurement are medium-size.

Contents

Introduction

Being diagnosed with having a food allergy or intolerance does not necessarily mean drastic changes in your diet. You'll need to be more careful in selecting foods and study labels thoroughly, but this will soon become second nature, and you'll see the benefits of a healthier diet.

What is the difference between an allergy and intolerance?
There is some confusion between a food allergy and intolerance, so it's important to establish which applies to you before deciding on treatment.

A food allergy occurs when a food triggers the body's immune system to react adversely, producing antibodies, usually within minutes and sometimes with side effects. Once the immune system has been primed to produce abnormal antibodies, the symptoms may be amplified the next time, causing severe allergic reactions to develop even with slight exposure.

Adverse reactions to foods can also be caused by intolerances. These occur when the body's digestive system is unable to digest foods properly, and the reactions are slower to develop and less severe than an allergy. Our bodies usually adapt to cope with a wide variety of foods, but when under stress, or on antibiotics, intolerances may develop.

What is celiac disease?
Celiac disease is an autoimmune disease, which occurs when the body's immune system reacts abnormally to gluten and produces antibodies that attack its own tissues. This causes inflammation and damage to the lining of the small intestine, which reduces the body's ability to absorb nutrients, causing symptoms such as anemia, osteoporosis, weight loss, painful abdominal bloating, and severe tiredness.

A blood test and biopsy can diagnose celiac disease, and a doctor or dietitian will advise on a strict gluten-free diet. Once foods containing gluten are removed from the diet, the damaged intestinal lining can recover and function properly; however, celiac disease is a lifelong condition, so you will need to restrict your diet permanently.

What is wheat allergy or intolerance?
Wheat allergy or intolerance can cause varied symptoms, including sinusitis, asthma, itchy and sore eyes, earache, headaches, migraine, muscle pain, stomach cramps, skin rashes, canker sores, coughing, tiredness, depression, bloating, flatulence, and nausea. Diagnosis involves blood and skin tests, and an exclusion diet is usually recommended.

What is dairy allergy or intolerance?
A dairy sensitivity is caused by an inability to digest lactose, a natural sugar in milk, or by casein, a milk protein. It often starts in childhood, but children may grow out of it. Symptoms vary, but include asthma, eczema, sinus problems, bloating, stomach pain, and digestive problems. Depending on the suspected cause, a blood, skin, or ingestion test is used for diagnosis, and treatment is by exclusion diet.

How to make sure you get vital nutrients
It's important to consult a doctor before restricting your diet, and it's vital to make

sure that you get all the essential nutrients by eating a good balance of food types.

When excluding gluten in wheat and other grains, a lack of the B vitamins, iron, and zinc can be made up by eating a selection of whole grains, such as rice, nuts, seeds, and beans, eggs, seafood, and variety meat. Soy products, avocadoes, dark green vegetables, and vegetable oils also supply vitamin E.

Dairy produce is a good source of protein, calcium, and vitamins A and B12, so a dairy-free diet should include green leafy vegetables, soy products, canned fish, beans, and cereals.

Gluten-, wheat-, dairy-free alternatives

Most supermarkets and health food stores stock a useful range of gluten-, wheat- and dairy-free alternatives for restricted diets.

Celiacs and those with wheat sensitivity can eat many other grains, including all varieties and forms of rice, buckwheat, amaranth, millet, quinoa, tapioca, sago, and corn. If you're sensitive to wheat, you can eat oats, barley, and rye.

Some celiacs can tolerate moderate amounts of oats, but you should make sure they are from an uncontaminated source, because there can be cross-contamination with other grains during processing at the mill.

Gluten-free flour, made from blends of rice, potato, tapioca, and buckwheat flours, is useful for home baking. Some flour blends have xanthan gum added for elasticity to improve texture in cakes. Single-grain flours, such as corn, rice, or chickpea (besan) flour can be used for thickening sauces, binding, or coating. Gluten-free pasta, breads, and unleavened crispbreads are also available.

Many dairy-free substitutes for milk and dairy products use soy, rice, nuts, quinoa, oats, or coconut. Olive, sunflower, soy, nut, and vegetable oils, and nondairy spreads are useful for cooking and spreading. Most people with lactose sensitivity will also react to goat's and sheep's milk.

Foods to watch out for

Always read labels on commercially prepared foods, because many contain hidden wheat, gluten, or dairy products or derivatives.

As well as ready-prepared meals, frozen meals, and burgers, many sauces, soups, bouillon cubes, mustard, spices, and some brands of baking powder may contain wheat. Potato chips and oven-baked French fries may have a wheat-base coating. Celiacs should also look for malt (from barley), used as a flavoring and coloring, and in beer-making. For people with dairy sensitivities, check for dairy-base ingredients in desserts, baked goods, chocolate, artificial sweeteners, and some vegetable oil spreads.

As always, before you start any new diet, consult your doctor first.

1

Breakfasts & Brunches

banana pancakes

serves 4

⅓ cup plus 1 tablespoon buckwheat flour

⅓ cup plus 1 tablespoon gluten-free all-purpose flour

pinch of salt

1 extra-large egg, lightly beaten

½ cup dairy-free milk

½ cup water

3 tablespoons dairy-free spread

maple syrup bananas

3 tablespoons dairy-free spread

2 tablespoons maple syrup

2 bananas, thickly sliced on the diagonal

Sift both types of flour and the salt into a mixing bowl. Make a well in the center and add the beaten egg, milk, and water. Using a balloon whisk, gradually mix the flour into the liquid ingredients, whisking well to get rid of any lumps, until you have a smooth batter.

Melt 5 teaspoons of the spread in a small saucepan and stir it into the batter. Pour the batter into a pitcher, cover, and let rest for 30 minutes.

Melt half of the remaining spread in a medium skillet. When the skillet is hot, pour in enough batter to make a thin pancake, swirling the skillet to achieve an even layer.

Cook one side until lightly brown, then, using a spatula, turn over and cook the other side. Slide onto a warm plate and cover with aluminum foil while you cook the remaining pancakes, adding more spread when needed.

To make the maple syrup bananas, wipe the skillet, add the spread, and heat until melted. Stir in the maple syrup, then add the bananas and cook for 2–3 minutes, or until the bananas have just softened and the sauce has thickened and caramelized. To serve, fold the thin pancakes in half and half again, then top with the bananas.

Calories: 363   Fat (of which saturated fat): 20 g (4 g)   Carbohydrate (of which sugar): 41 g (19 g)   Salt: 0.7 g

apple granola

makes 10 portions

½ cup sunflower seeds

¼ cup pumpkin seeds

¾ cup coarsely chopped hazelnuts

2½ cups buckwheat flakes

2½ cups rice flakes

3 cups millet flakes

1⅓ cups coarsely chopped plumped dried apple

¾ cup coarsely chopped dried pitted dates

Heat a dry skillet over medium heat, add the seeds and hazelnuts, and lightly toast, shaking the skillet frequently, for 4 minutes, or until golden brown. Transfer to a large mixing bowl and let cool.

Add the flakes, apple, and dates to the bowl and mix thoroughly until combined. Store the granola in an airtight jar or container.

Calories: 322   Fat (of which saturated fat): 12 g (1.5 g)   Carbohydrate (of which sugar): 44 g (14.5 g)   Salt: Trace

hot oatmeal

serves 4

5½ cups millet flakes

2 cups dairy-free milk

pinch of salt

freshly grated nutmeg

apricot puree

1 cup coarsely chopped plumped dried apricots

1¼ cups water

To make the apricot puree, put the apricots into a saucepan and cover with the water. Bring to a boil, then reduce the heat and simmer, half covered, for 20 minutes, until the apricots are tender. Transfer the apricots, along with any water left in the saucepan, to a food processor or blender and process until smooth. Set aside.

To make the oatmeal, put the millet flakes into a saucepan and add the milk and salt. Bring to a boil, then reduce the heat and simmer for 5 minutes, stirring frequently, until cooked and creamy.

To serve, spoon into four bowls and top with the apricot puree and a little nutmeg.

Calories: 289   Fat (of which saturated fat): 3 g (1 g)   Carbohydrate (of which sugar): 52 g (12 g)   Salt: 0.6 g

berry crunch

serves 4

1½ cups rice, buckwheat, or millet flakes, or a mixture

¼ cup honey

2¼ cups thick, plain soy yogurt or dairy-free alternative

finely grated rind of 1 orange

2 cups frozen mixed berries, such as raspberries, blackberries, and blueberries, partly thawed, plus extra to decorate

Heat a dry skillet over medium heat, add the flakes, and toast, shaking the skillet, for 1 minute. Add half of the honey and stir to coat the flakes. Cook, stirring continuously, until the flakes turn golden brown and slightly crisp.

Put the yogurt into a bowl and stir in the remaining honey and the orange rind. Gently stir in the berries, reserving a few to decorate. Let stand for 10–15 minutes for the berries to release their juices, then stir again to create a swirl of color.

To serve, spoon a layer of flakes into the bottom of four glasses, then top with a layer of the berry yogurt. Sprinkle with another layer of flakes and add another layer of the yogurt. Decorate with the reserved berries.

Calories: 225   Fat (of which saturated fat): 4 g (2.5 g)   Carbohydrate (of which sugar): 37 g (23 g)   Salt: 0.3 g

peach puree

serves 4

4 peaches or nectarines, pitted

3 tablespoons orange juice

12 ounces soft silken tofu, drained (about 1⅓ cups)

2 tablespoons maple syrup

⅓ cup walnut pieces, coarsely chopped

1 tablespoon demerara sugar or other raw sugar

Coarsely chop the peaches and puree with a handheld blender or in a food processor until smooth. Add the orange juice and blend again.

Process the tofu with a handheld blender or in a food processor until smooth. Stir in the maple syrup.

Place alternate tablespoonfuls of the fruit puree and tofu mixture into four tall stemmed glasses or individual dishes, swirling lightly to create a marbled effect.

Mix together the walnuts and sugar, then spoon on top of the peach purees just before serving.

Calories: 252   Fat (of which saturated fat): 12 g (1.5 g)   Carbohydrate (of which sugar): 17.5 g (16 g)   Salt: Trace

banana smoothie

serves 4

1 cup whole blanched almonds

2½ cups dairy-free milk

2 ripe bananas, halved

1 teaspoon natural vanilla extract

ground cinnamon, for sprinkling

Put the almonds into a food processor and process until very finely chopped. Add the milk, bananas, and vanilla extract and blend until smooth and creamy.

Pour into glasses and sprinkle with cinnamon.

Calories: 314   Fat (of which saturated fat): 22.5 g (1.5 g)   Carbohydrate (of which sugar): 15 g (11 g)   Salt: Trace

strawberry shake

serves 4

7 ounces strawberries,
hulled, plus 4 whole
strawberries, to decorate

1¼ cups seedless
green grapes

¾ cup unsweetened
soy milk

2 tablespoons almond
butter, or peanut butter

1 tablespoon honey

1 tablespoon sesame seeds

Place the strawberries, grapes, milk, almond butter, and honey in a food processor or blender and process until smooth.

Dip the whole strawberries halfway into the shake mixture, then dip into the sesame seeds.

Pour the shake into four glasses and top each with a sesame-dipped strawberry to serve.

Calories: 140   Fat (of which saturated fat): 7 g (1.5 g)   Carbohydrate (of which sugar): 15 g (15 g)   Salt: Trace

blueberry bars

makes 12

sunflower oil, for greasing

¾ cup gluten-free all-purpose flour

1⅛ teaspoons gluten-free baking powder

⅛ teaspoon salt

½ cup quinoa flakes

3½ cups puffed rice

½ cup slivered almonds

1½ cups blueberries

⅓ cup plus 1 tablespoon dairy-free soy spread

⅓ cup plus 1 tablespoon honey

1 egg, beaten

Preheat the oven to 350°F. Grease an 11 x 7-inch rectangular baking pan and line the bottom with nonstick parchment paper.

Sift the flour, baking powder, and salt into a mixing bowl, add the quinoa, puffed rice, almonds, and blueberries, and mix together. Place the soy spread and honey in a saucepan and heat gently until just melted, then stir evenly into the dry ingredients with the egg.

Spread the batter into the prepared pan, smoothing with a spatula. Bake in the oven for 25–30 minutes, until golden brown and firm.

Let cool in the pan for 15 minutes, then cut into 12 bars. Transfer to a wire rack to continue cooling.

Calories: 277   Fat (of which saturated fat): 13 g (2.5 g)   Carbohydrate (of which sugar): 21 g (10 g)   Salt: 0.3 g

plum pancakes

serves 6

8 red plums, pitted and cut into quarters

½ cup maple syrup

1 tablespoon lemon juice

1 piece star anise

1⅔ cups gluten-free and wheat-free flour blend

1½ teaspoons gluten-free baking powder

2 eggs, beaten

¾ cup plus 2 tablespoons sweetened soy milk

½ cup plain soy yogurt

1 tablespoon sunflower oil, plus extra for greasing

Place the plums, syrup, lemon juice, and star anise in a saucepan and heat until almost boiling. Reduce the heat, cover, and cook gently for 8–10 minutes, stirring occasionally, until tender.

Place the flour, baking powder, eggs, milk, yogurt, and oil in a blender or food processor and blend to a smooth, bubbly batter.

Lightly grease a large, heavy skillet or griddle pan and heat until hot. Drop tablespoonfuls of the batter onto the skillet and cook for 5–6 minutes, turning once, until golden and set. Cook in batches to make about 24 pancakes.

To serve, stack four pancakes on each plate and spoon over the plums and juices.

Calories: 266   Fat (of which saturated fat): 8 g (1.5 g)   Carbohydrate (of which sugar): 42.5 g (16.5 g)   Salt: 0.6 g

potato pancakes

serves 4

½ cup cold
mashed potatoes

¾ cup plus 2 tablespoons
dairy-free milk

⅔ cup gluten-free
all-purpose flour

1 teaspoon gluten-free
baking powder

⅛ teaspoon salt

1 egg, beaten

sunflower oil, for frying

to serve

8 good-quality bacon strips,
cooked until crisp

1½ tablespoons
maple syrup

Put the mashed potatoes and milk into a food processor or blender and process to a thin puree.

Sift the flour, baking powder, and salt into a mixing bowl, make a well in the center of the flour, and add the beaten egg and potato puree. Using a balloon whisk, gradually mix the flour into the liquid ingredients, whisking well to make a smooth, creamy, thick batter.

Heat a little oil in a large, nonstick skillet. Pour a tablespoonful of batter per cake into the skillet—you will probably fit about three in the skillet at one time. Cook each cake for 2 minutes on each side, until golden brown. Remove from the skillet and keep warm while you cook the remaining potato cakes.

Divide the cakes among four warm plates, top each serving with two bacon strips, and drizzle with maple syrup.

Calories: 276   Fat (of which saturated fat): 15 g (4 g)   Carbohydrate (of which sugar): 21.5 g (4 g)   Salt: 2.3 g

chickpea fritters

serves 4

1 cup gluten-free all-purpose flour

1½ teaspoons gluten-free baking powder

⅛ teaspoon salt

1 egg, beaten

¾ cup unsweetened soy milk

2½ cups thinly sliced scallions

1⅔ cups rinsed and drained canned chickpeas (garbanzo beans)

¼ cup chopped cilantro

sunflower oil, for frying

salt and pepper

cilantro sprigs, to garnish

Sift the flour, baking powder, and salt into a mixing bowl and make a well in the center. Add the egg and milk and stir into the flour, then beat to make a smooth batter.

Stir in the scallions, chickpeas, and cilantro, then season well with salt and pepper.

Heat the oil in a large, heavy skillet and add tablespoonfuls of the batter. Cook in batches for 4–5 minutes, turning once, until golden brown.

Serve the fritters stacked on warmed serving plates, garnished with cilantro sprigs.

Calories: 250   Fat (of which saturated fat): 6 g (0.8 g)   Carbohydrate (of which sugar): 36 g (4 g)   Salt: 0.3 g

sausage frittata

serves 4

4 gluten-free sausages or vegetarian alternative

sunflower oil, for frying

4 boiled potatoes, cooled and diced

8 cherry tomatoes

4 eggs, beaten

salt and pepper

Preheat the broiler to medium–high. Arrange the sausages on a foil-lined broiler pan and cook under the preheated broiler, turning occasionally, for 12–15 minutes, or until cooked through and golden brown. Let cool slightly, then slice into bite-size pieces.

Meanwhile, heat a little oil in a medium (10-inch), heavy skillet with an ovenproof handle over medium heat. Add the potatoes and cook until golden brown and crisp all over, then add the tomatoes and cook for an additional 2 minutes. Arrange the sausages in the skillet so that there is an even distribution of potatoes, tomatoes, and sausages.

Add a little more oil to the skillet if it seems dry. Season the beaten eggs to taste with salt and pepper and pour the mixture over the ingredients in the skillet. Cook for 3 minutes, without stirring or disturbing the eggs. Place the skillet under the preheated broiler for 3 minutes, or until the top is just cooked. Cut into wedges to serve.

Calories: 137   Fat (of which saturated fat): 6.5 g (2 g)   Carbohydrate (of which sugar): 13 g (3 g)   Salt: 0.5 g

eggs & fritters

serves 4

10½ ounces celeriac, peeled

1 small onion

3 tablespoons chopped fresh parsley

4 portobello mushrooms (about 3½ ounces)

¼ cup olive oil

4 eggs

2 tbsp unsweetened soy milk

salt and pepper

Preheat the oven to 400°F. Coarsely grate the celeriac and onion in a food processor or by hand. Add 2 tablespoons of the parsley and season well.

Place the mushrooms on a baking sheet, brush with about 1 tablespoon of oil, and season with salt and pepper. Bake for 10–12 minutes.

Heat 2 tablespoons of the oil in a large, heavy skillet. Place four large spoonfuls of the celeriac mixture in the skillet, pressing with a spatula to flatten. Cook for about 10 minutes, turning once, until golden. Drain on paper towels and keep hot.

Meanwhile, beat the eggs with the milk, remaining parsley, and salt and pepper. Heat the remaining oil in a small saucepan and cook the egg, stirring, until just set.

Place the fritters on warm serving plates, top each with a mushroom, and spoon over the scrambled eggs.

Calories: 213   Fat (of which saturated fat): 18 g (3.4 g)   Carbohydrate (of which sugar): 3.5 g (2.5 g)   Salt: 0.4 g

cornbread & avocado

serves 4

¼ cup olive oil,
plus extra for greasing

1 cup medium cornmeal

1 cup plus 3 tablespoons
soy flour

1 tablespoon gluten-free
baking powder

⅓ cup snipped chives

1 extra-large egg, beaten

1½ cups unsweetened
soy milk

8 pancetta slices or
8 wafer-thin ham slices

1 ripe avocado

salt and pepper

Preheat the oven to 375°F. Grease a 7-inch square shallow cake pan with oil.

Sift the cornmeal, flour, baking powder, and salt and pepper into a bowl. Stir in the chives.

Beat together the egg, milk, and oil and stir into the dry ingredients, mixing evenly. Spoon the mixture into the pan and smooth the top with a spatula.

Bake for 30–35 minutes, or until firm and golden. Meanwhile, place the pancetta slices on a baking sheet and bake for 10–12 minutes, until golden and crisp. Drain on paper towels.

Halve, pit, and slice the avocado. Cut the cornbread into four squares and serve warm, topped with pancetta and avocado.

| Calories: 590 | Fat (of which saturated fat): 39 g (8.5 g) | Carbohydrate (of which sugar): 30 g (3.5 g) | Salt: 2.8 g |

broccoli hash

serves 4

3–4 medium mealy potatoes, such as russets or Yukon Gold, cut into ½-inch cubes (2⅔ cups)

2½ cups small broccoli florets

2 tablespoons sunflower oil

1 onion, finely chopped

1 large red bell pepper, cut into small dice

¼–½ teaspoon crushed red pepper

4 extra-large eggs

salt and pepper

Cook the potatoes in lightly salted boiling water for 6 minutes. Drain well. Blanch or steam the broccoli for 3 minutes.

Heat the oil in a large skillet over high heat, add the onion and red bell pepper, and sauté for 2–3 minutes to soften. Add the potatoes and cook, turning occasionally, for 6–8 minutes, until tender.

Stir in the broccoli and crushed red pepper, then cook over low heat, turning the mixture occasionally, until golden brown. Season to taste with salt and pepper.

Meanwhile, bring a wide saucepan of water to just simmering point. Break the eggs into the water and poach gently for 3–4 minutes, until softly set.

Spoon the hash onto warm plates and top each portion with a poached egg.

Calories: 260   Fat (of which saturated fat): 13.9 g (2.8 g)   Carbohydrate (of which sugar): 20.9 g (4.7 g)   Salt: 0.27 g

stir-fried vegetables

serves 4

6½ cups gluten-free vegetable stock

2 tablespoons wheat- and gluten-free soy sauce

2 garlic cloves, thinly sliced

1-inch piece ginger, thinly sliced

1 cinnamon stick

1 bay leaf

1 carrot, thinly shredded

1 small fennel bulb, thinly sliced

5½ ounces vermicelli rice noodles

1¼ cups sliced white mushrooms

1 cup bean sprouts

4 scallions, sliced

3 tablespoons chopped cilantro

handful of basil leaves

chopped red chiles, lime wedges, and wheat- and gluten-free soy sauce

Place the stock in a large saucepan with the soy sauce, garlic, ginger, cinnamon, and bay leaf. Bring to a boil, reduce the heat, cover, and simmer for about 20 minutes.

Add the carrot and fennel and simmer for 1 minute. Add the noodles and simmer for an additional 4 minutes.

Add the mushrooms, bean sprouts, and scallions and return to a boil.

Ladle into soup bowls and sprinkle with cilantro and basil leaves. Serve with chiles, lime wedges, and soy sauce at the table.

Calories: 182   Fat (of which saturated fat): 1.2 g (0.1 g)   Carbohydrate (of which sugar): 32.8 g (3.8 g)   Salt: 1.4 g

soda bread

makes 1 loaf (serves 6)

5 plumped pitted dried plums (prunes), chopped

16 plumped dried apricot halves, chopped

½ cup chopped dried apples

⅓ cup dried cranberries

⅔ cup apple juice

2 tablespoons sunflower oil, plus extra for greasing

3¾ cups gluten- and wheat-free baking flour blend

1½ tablespoons gluten-free baking powder

2 teaspoons xanthan gum

¼ teaspoon salt

1 cup soy milk, plus extra for brushing

¼ cup maple syrup

1 tablespoon pumpkin seeds

Place the dried plums, apricots, apples, and cranberries in a bowl and pour over the apple juice. Cover and let stand for about 30 minutes.

Preheat the oven to 400°F. Brush a baking sheet with oil. Sift the flour, baking powder, xanthan gum, and salt into a bowl and make a well in the center. Mix the oil, milk, and maple syrup and add to the dry ingredients with the fruits and juice, mixing lightly to a soft, but not sticky, dough. Add a little more milk if the dough feels dry.

Shape the dough to a smooth circle on the prepared baking sheet, flatten slightly, and cut a deep cross through the center almost to the bottom. Gently pull the wedges apart at the points. Brush with milk and sprinkle with pumpkin seeds.

Bake in the preheated oven for 25–30 minutes, or until golden brown and the bottom sounds hollow when tapped.

Calories: 427   Fat (of which saturated fat): 7 g (1 g)   Carbohydrate (of which sugar): 84 g (20 g)   Salt: 1.5 g

sunflower muffins

makes 12

2½ cups gluten-and wheat-free baking flour blend

4 teaspoons gluten-free baking powder

½ teaspoon xanthan gum

1 teaspoon ground allspice

⅔ cup firmly packed light brown sugar

¼ cup sunflower seeds

1⅔ cups grated carrots

finely grated rind and juice 1 small orange

2 eggs, beaten

⅔ cup unsweetened soy milk

⅓ cup plus 2 tablespoons sunflower oil

1 teaspoon vanilla extract

Preheat the oven to 400°F. Place 12 baking cups into a muffin pan.

Sift the flour, baking powder, xanthan gum, and allspice into a large bowl. Stir in the sugar with 3 tablespoons of the sunflower seeds, the carrots, and orange rind.

Lightly beat together the orange juice, eggs, milk, oil, and vanilla with a fork and stir into the dry ingredients, mixing to make a batter—it will be a little lumpy.

Spoon the batter into the baking cups and sprinkle with the remaining sunflower seeds. Bake in the oven for about 20 minutes, or until well risen and golden brown. Serve warm.

Calories: 231   Fat (of which saturated fat): 9.5 g (1.5 g)   Carbohydrate (of which sugar): 35 g (13 g)   Salt: 0.7 g

Light Lunches

potato salad

serves 6

1 pound 2 ounces
new potatoes

16 vine-ripened cherry
tomatoes, halved

12 ripe black olives, pitted
and coarsely chopped

4 scallions, sliced

2 tablespoons chopped
fresh mint

2 tablespoons chopped
fresh parsley

2 tablespoons chopped
fresh cilantro

juice of 1 lemon

3 tablespoons extra virgin
olive oil

salt and pepper

Cook the potatoes in a saucepan of lightly salted boiling water for 15 minutes, or until tender. Drain, then let cool slightly before peeling off the skins. Cut into halves or quarters, depending on the size of the potato, then combine with the tomatoes, olives, scallions, and herbs in a salad bowl.

Mix the lemon juice and oil together in a small bowl or pitcher and pour over the potato salad. Season to taste with salt and pepper before serving.

Calories: 140   Fat (of which saturated fat): 8 g (1 g)   Carbohydrate (of which sugar): 15 g (3 g)   Salt: 0.2 g

onion soup

serves 4

7 red onions (about 1¾ pounds), peeled and quartered

1 tablespoon olive oil

1 tablespoon dairy-free spread

1 cup dry white wine

5 cups gluten-free vegetable stock

1 fresh rosemary sprig, plus extra to garnish

1 teaspoon chopped fresh thyme

1 teaspoon Dijon mustard

salt and pepper

croutons

1¼ cups water

⅓ cup fine instant polenta

½ teaspoon salt

1 tablespoon chopped fresh rosemary

olive oil, for brushing

Preheat the oven to 400°F. Put the onions and oil into a roasting pan and toss well. Dot with the spread, season to taste with salt, and roast in the preheated oven for 45 minutes. Remove from the oven and let cool slightly.

Discard the outer layer of each onion segment if crisp, then cut the remainder into thick slices. Put the onions into a large, heavy saucepan with the wine and bring to a boil. Cook until most of the wine has evaporated. Stir in the stock and herbs and cook over medium–low heat for 30–35 minutes, or until reduced and thickened. Stir in the mustard and season to taste with salt and pepper.

Meanwhile, to make the polenta croutons, heat the water to boiling point in a saucepan. Pour in the polenta in a steady stream and cook, stirring continuously with a wooden spoon, for 5 minutes, or until thickened. Stir in the salt and rosemary. Cover a cutting board with a sheet of plastic wrap, then, using a spatula, spread out the polenta in an even layer about ½ inch thick. Let cool and firm up. Cut into bite-size cubes, brush with oil, and arrange on a baking sheet. Cook in the oven, turning occasionally, for 10–15 minutes, or until crisp and lightly golden brown. Remove the rosemary from the soup and discard. Transfer half of the soup to a food processor or blender and process until smooth, then return to the saucepan and stir well. To serve, ladle into four warm bowls and top with the polenta croutons and sprigs of rosemary.

Calories: 238   Fat (of which saturated fat): 7.4 g (1 g)   Carbohydrate (of which sugar): 25.4 g (11.1 g)   Salt: 0.68 g

golden pilaf

serves 4

2 cups gluten-free vegetable or chicken stock

1¼ cups toasted buckwheat

3 tablespoons olive oil

1 onion, sliced

2 garlic cloves, thinly sliced

¾-inch piece ginger, thinly sliced

½ teaspoon ground turmeric

½ teaspoon ground cinnamon

¼ cup orange juice

½ cup raisins

2 carrots, coarsely shredded

⅓ cup pine nuts, toasted

salt and pepper

shreds of orange zest and cilantro, to garnish

Bring the stock to a boil and add the buckwheat. Simmer for 5–6 minutes, until most of the liquid is absorbed, then add 1 tablespoon of the oil, cover, and let cook over low heat for 10 minutes, until tender.

Heat the remaining oil and sauté the onion over medium heat for 5–6 minutes, stirring occasionally, until soft and golden brown.

Add the garlic and ginger and stir for 1 minute, then stir in the turmeric, cinnamon, orange juice, and raisins and cook for 1 minute.

Add the carrots, cooked buckwheat, and pine nuts, stirring until evenly heated. Season to taste with salt and pepper.

Pile the pilaf onto a warm serving plate and scatter over the orange zest and cilantro. Serve either on its own or as an accompaniment to broiled or roasted meats.

Calories: 446   Fat (of which saturated fat): 19 g (2 g)   Carbohydrate (of which sugar): 60 g (21 g)   Salt: 0.2 g

risotto pie

serves 6

1 tablespoon olive oil,
plus extra for greasing

1 cup Arborio
risotto rice

2 cups gluten-free chicken
or vegetable stock

½ cup coconut milk

8 scallions,
thinly sliced

8 ounces fresh baby
spinach leaves

2 eggs, beaten

2 tablespoons chopped
cilantro

salt and pepper

mixed salad greens,
to serve

Preheat the oven to 400°F. Brush a 9-inch cake pan with oil and line the bottom with nonstick parchment paper.

Heat the oil in a large saucepan, add the rice, and cook, stirring, for 1 minute. Add a ladleful of stock and cook, stirring often, until the liquid is almost absorbed. Continue to add the stock gradually until the rice is almost tender and there is no free liquid. Stir in the coconut milk and scallions and season well with salt and pepper. Remove from the heat.

Meanwhile, place the spinach in a saucepan with just the water clinging to its leaves after rinsing and heat until the leaves are wilted. Drain, pressing out any free liquid. Stir into the rice with the beaten eggs and chopped cilantro.

Transfer the mixture to the prepared cake pan, smoothing the top, and bake for 25–30 minutes, until just set. Invert and serve hot or cold, cut into wedges, with salad greens.

Calories: 345   Fat (of which saturated fat): 14 g (6 g)   Carbohydrate (of which sugar): 41 g (2.5 g)   Salt: 0.3 g

bruschettas

serves 4

2 tablespoons olive oil,
plus extra for brushing

2 cups water

½ cup plus 1 tablespoon
instant polenta

16 cherry vine tomatoes

salt and pepper

tapenade

12 sun-dried tomato pieces,
soaked and drained

8 pitted ripe black olives

2 tablespoons salted
capers, rinsed

2 tablespoons chopped flat-
leaf parsley

1 garlic clove, crushed

juice of ½ lemon

2 tablespoons extra virgin
olive oil

salt and pepper

Preheat the broiler to high. Grease a 9-inch loaf pan with oil. Place the water in a large saucepan with a pinch of salt and bring to a boil.

Sprinkle in the polenta and stir continuously over moderate heat for about 5 minutes, until thick and smooth. Remove from the heat, stir in the oil and salt and pepper to taste, then spread into the prepared pan. Let stand to set.

To make the tapenade, finely chop the sun-dried tomatoes, olives, capers, and parsley. Mix with the garlic, lemon juice, and oil, and season with salt and pepper to taste.

Cut the polenta into eight slices and arrange on a baking sheet with the cherry vine tomatoes. Brush with oil and broil until golden, turning once.

Serve the polenta slices topped with a spoonful of tapenade and the broiled tomatoes.

Calories: 280   Fat (of which saturated fat): 20 g (3 g)   Carbohydrate (of which sugar): 19 g (1.5 g)   Salt: 0.9 g

tabbouleh

serves 4

1¼ cups quinoa

2½ cups water

10 vine-ripened cherry tomatoes, halved

3-inch piece cucumber, diced

3 scallions, sliced

juice of ½ lemon

2 tablespoons extra virgin olive oil

¼ cup chopped fresh mint

¼ cup chopped fresh cilantro

¼ cup chopped fresh parsley

salt and pepper

Put the quinoa into a medium saucepan and cover with the water. Bring to a boil, then reduce the heat, cover, and simmer over low heat for 15 minutes, or according to the package directions. Drain if necessary.

Let the quinoa cool slightly before combining with the remaining ingredients in a salad bowl. Season to taste with salt and pepper before serving.

| Calories: 200 | Fat (of which saturated fat): 8 g (1 g) | Carbohydrate (of which sugar): 25 g (5 g) | Salt: 0.1 g |

bacon & pear salad

serves 4

4 lean bacon strips

⅔ cup walnut halves

2 red Bartlett pears, cored and sliced lengthwise

1 tablespoon lemon juice

6 ounces watercress, tough stems removed

dressing

3 tablespoons extra virgin olive oil

2 tablespoons lemon juice

½ teaspoon honey

salt and pepper

Preheat the broiler to high. Arrange the bacon on an aluminum foil-lined broiler pan and cook under the preheated broiler until brown and crisp. Set aside to cool, then cut into ½-inch pieces.

Meanwhile, heat a dry skillet over medium heat and lightly toast the walnuts, shaking the skillet frequently, for 3 minutes, or until lightly brown. Set aside to cool.

Toss the pears in the lemon juice to prevent discoloration. Put the watercress, walnuts, pears, and bacon into a salad bowl.

To make the dressing, whisk the oil, lemon juice, and honey together in a small bowl or pitcher. Season to taste with salt and pepper, then pour over the salad. Toss well to combine and serve.

Calories: 280   Fat (of which saturated fat): 23 g (3 g)   Carbohydrate (of which sugar): 9 g (9 g)   Salt: 0.9 g

spicy carrot soup

serves 4

2 tablespoons olive oil

1 large onion, chopped

1 celery stalk, chopped

1 potato, diced

6 carrots, sliced

1 teaspoon paprika

2 teaspoons ground cumin

1 teaspoon ground coriander

½ teaspoon chili powder (optional)

1 cup red lentils

5 cups gluten-free vegetable or chicken stock

2 bay leaves

salt and pepper

2 tablespoons chopped fresh cilantro, to garnish

Heat the oil in a large, heavy saucepan over medium–low heat. Add the onion and cook for 7 minutes, stirring occasionally. Add the celery, potato, and carrots and cook for an additional 5 minutes, stirring occasionally. Stir in the paprika, cumin, ground coriander, and chili powder, if using, and cook for another minute.

Stir in the lentils, stock, and bay leaves. Bring to a boil, then reduce the heat and simmer, covered halfway, over low heat, stirring occasionally to prevent the lentils from sticking to the bottom of the saucepan, for 25 minutes, or until the lentils are tender.

Remove and discard the bay leaves. Transfer to a food processor or blender, or use a handhend blender, and process the soup until thick and smooth. Return to the saucepan and reheat. Season to taste with salt and pepper and add extra chili powder, if liked. Ladle into four warm bowls and sprinkle with fresh cilantro before serving.

Calories: 290   Fat (of which saturated fat): 7 g (1 g)   Carbohydrate (of which sugar): 46 g (14 g)   Salt: 0.15 g

tofu & noodle salad

serves 4

7 ounces buckwheat
noodles

9 ounces firm smoked tofu

2 cups finely shredded
green cabbage

2¼ cups finely
shredded carrots

3 scallions, diagonally sliced

1 fresh red chile, seeded
and finely sliced

2 tablespoons sesame
seeds, lightly toasted,
to garnish

dressing

1 teaspoon grated fresh
ginger

1 garlic clove, crushed

6 ounces silken tofu

4 teaspoons wheat- and
gluten-free soy sauce

2 tablespoons sesame oil

¼ cup hot water

salt

Cook the noodles in a large saucepan of lightly salted boiling water according to the package directions. Drain and refresh under cold running water.

To make the dressing, blend the ginger, garlic, silken tofu, soy sauce, oil, and water together in a small bowl until smooth and creamy. Season to taste with salt.

Place the smoked tofu in a steamer. Steam for 5 minutes, then cut into thin slices.

Meanwhile, put the cabbage, carrots, scallions, and chile into a bowl and toss to mix. To serve, arrange the noodles on serving plates and top with the carrot salad and slices of tofu. Spoon over the dressing and garnish with sesame seeds.

Calories: 435   Fat (of which saturated fat): 20 g (4 g)   Carbohydrate (of which sugar): 43 g (9 g)   Salt: 1 g

chicken tacos

serves 4

1 ripe avocado

⅔ cup plain soy yogurt

2 tablespoons medium cornmeal

1 teaspoon chili powder

½ teaspoon dried thyme

1¼ pounds chicken breasts, cut into thin strips

2 tablespoons sunflower oil

1 red onion, sliced

1 large red bell pepper, seeded and sliced

1 large green bell pepper, seeded and sliced

8 wheat- and gluten-free taco shells

salt and pepper

smoked paprika, to garnish

Halve the avocado, remove the pit, and scoop out the flesh, then puree in a blender with the yogurt. Season to taste with salt and pepper.

Mix together the cornmeal, chili powder, and thyme with salt and pepper in a large bowl. Add the chicken and toss to coat evenly.

Heat the oil in a wok or large skillet and stir-fry the onion and peppers for 3–4 minutes to soften. Remove and keep hot.

Add the chicken and stir-fry for 5–6 minutes, until evenly browned. Return the vegetables to the pan and stir-fry for an additional 1–2 minutes.

Spoon the chicken mixture into the taco shells and top with a spoonful of the avocado mixture. Sprinkle with smoked paprika and serve.

Calories: 465   Fat (of which saturated fat): 21 g (3 g)   Carbohydrate (of which sugar): 25 g (8 g)   Salt: 0.3 g

spring rolls

makes 16 rolls

2 tablespoons wheat- and gluten-free soy sauce

1½ teaspoons maple syrup

1 pound 2 ounces lean pork tenderloin

vegetable oil, for frying

32 rice paper wrappers

gluten-free hoisin sauce

2½ ounces rice vermicelli noodles, cooked

strips of cucumber

strips of scallion

Blend the soy sauce and maple syrup together in a shallow dish. Add the pork and turn to coat in the mixture. Cover and let marinate in the refrigerator for at least 1 hour or preferably overnight.

Heat a ridged grill pan over medium–high heat until hot, add a little oil to cover the bottom, and cook the pork for 4–6 minutes on each side, depending on the thickness of the meat, until cooked and caramelized on the outside. Remove from the pan and slice into fine strips.

Fill a heatproof bowl with water that is almost boiling. Put two rice paper wrappers on top of one another (you will need two per spring roll because they are thin and fragile) and soak in the water for 20 seconds, or until they turn pliable and opaque. Carefully remove the wrappers, using a spatula, drain for a second, and place flat on a plate.

Spread a spoonful of hoisin sauce over a pair of rice paper wrappers and top with a small bundle of noodles and a few strips of pork, cucumber, and scallion. Fold in the ends and sides of the wrappers to resemble a spring roll. Set aside while you make the remaining rolls. Slice in half on the diagonal and serve with a little more hoisin sauce, if liked.

Calories: 96   Fat (of which saturated fat): 3 g (0.5 g)   Carbohydrate (of which sugar): 8 g (1 g)   Salt: 0.4 g

sushi rolls

serves 4

4 sheets nori (seaweed)

wasabi (Japanese horseradish sauce)

wheat- and gluten-free soy sauce

pink pickled ginger

rice

1⅓ cups glutinous rice or short-grain white rice

2 tablespoons rice vinegar

1 teaspoon sugar

½ teaspoon salt

fillings

1¾ ounces smoked salmon

1½-inch piece cucumber, peeled, seeded, and cut into matchsticks

1½ ounces cooked peeled shrimp

1 small avocado, pitted, peeled, thinly sliced, and tossed in lemon juice

Put the rice into a saucepan and cover with cold water. Bring to a boil, then reduce the heat, cover, and simmer for 15–20 minutes, or according to the package directions, until the rice is tender and the water has been absorbed. Drain if necessary and transfer to a bowl. Mix the vinegar, sugar, and salt together, then, using a spatula, stir well into the rice. Cover with a damp cloth and let cool.

To make the rolls, lay a bamboo mat over a cutting board. Lay a sheet of nori, shiny side down, on the mat. Spread one-fourth of the rice mixture over the nori, using wet fingers to press it down evenly, leaving a ½-inch margin at the top and bottom.

For smoked salmon and cucumber rolls, lay the salmon over the rice and arrange the cucumber in a line across the center. For the shrimp rolls, lay the shrimp and avocado in a line across the center.

Carefully hold the nearest edge of the mat, then, using the mat as a guide, roll up the nori tightly to make a neat tube of rice enclosing the filling. Seal the uncovered edge with a little water, then roll the sushi off the mat. Repeat to make three more rolls—you need two salmon and cucumber and two shrimp-and-avocado rolls in total. Using a wet knife, cut each roll into eight pieces and stand upright on a platter. Wipe and rinse the knife between cuts to prevent the rice from sticking. Serve the rolls with wasabi, soy sauce, and pickled ginger.

| Calories: 312 | Fat (of which saturated fat): 6.5 g (1 g) | Carbohydrate (of which sugar): 48 g (1.5 g) | Salt: 1.1 g |

seafood pizza

serves 4

2 tablespoons olive oil, plus extra for greasing

1⅔ cups buckwheat flour

⅔ cup rice flour

¾ cup plus 2 tablespoons potato flour

2 teaspoons xanthan gum

2¼ teaspoons gluten-free fast-action yeast

1 teaspoon salt

1½ cups lukewarm water

¾ cup tomato puree

2 shallots, finely chopped

2 tablespoons chopped fresh dill

one 6-ounce can tuna in oil, drained and flaked

6 ounces jumbo shrimp, cooked and peeled

10 ounces artichokes in oil, drained

2 tablespoons capers, rinsed

8 pitted black or green olives

salt and pepper

Brush a large baking sheet with oil. Mix the flours, xanthan gum, yeast, and salt in a bowl, make a well in the center, and stir in the water with 1 tablespoon of oil to make a soft dough.

Knead the dough gently on a lightly floured surface for 4–5 minutes, until smooth, then roll to a 13-inch circle on the prepared baking sheet, pushing the edges up slightly to make a raised edge. Cover and let stand in a warm place for about 1½ hours, or until risen and doubled in size.

Preheat the oven to 400°F. Spread the tomato puree over the dough to within ½ inch of the edge. Sprinkle over the shallots and 1 tablespoon of dill. Top with the tuna, shrimp, artichokes, capers, and olives. Season with salt and pepper and sprinkle with the remaining oil.

Bake in the preheated oven for 25–30 minutes. Sprinkle with the remaining dill and serve hot.

Calories: 621   Fat (of which saturated fat): 19 g (2.5 g)   Carbohydrate (of which sugar): 81 g (2.5 g)   Salt: 3.7 g

baba ghanoush

serves 6

1 large eggplant, pricked

3 fat garlic cloves, unpeeled

1 teaspoon ground coriander

1 teaspoon ground cumin

1 tablespoon light tahini

juice of ½ lemon

2 tablespoons extra virgin olive oil

salt and pepper

cilantro, to garnish

flat breads

2 cups gluten-free white bread flour

2 tablespoons fine cornmeal

1 teaspoon gluten-free baking powder

1 teaspoon salt

3½ tablespoons dairy-free spread, diced

1 tablespoon sesame seeds

⅔–¾ cup warm water

sunflower oil, for oiling

To make the baba ghanoush dip, preheat the oven to 400°F. Put the eggplant into a roasting pan and bake in the preheated oven for 25 minutes. Add the garlic cloves to the roasting pan and cook for an additional 15 minutes, until the eggplant and garlic are tender.

Halve the eggplant and, using a spoon, scoop out the flesh into a food processor or blender. Peel the garlic cloves and add to the food processor or blender with the spices, tahini, lemon juice, and oil. Process until smooth and creamy, then season to taste with salt and pepper. Transfer to a serving dish and cover until required.

Meanwhile, make the flat breads. Sift the flour, cornmeal, baking powder, and salt into a bowl, then rub in the spread until the mixture resembles bread crumbs. Add the sesame seeds and stir in the water with your hands to form the mixture into a ball, adding more water or flour if needed.

Turn the mixture out onto a lightly floured surface and knead lightly until a soft dough forms. Divide into six pieces, then roll each piece into a ball. Wrap in plastic wrap and let rest in the refrigerator for 30 minutes. Roll out or press the dough balls with your fingers into ¼-inch thick circles. Heat a lightly oiled ridged grill pan over medium heat and cook each flat bread for a few minutes on each side until lightly golden. Garnish the baba ghanoush with cilantro and serve with the warm flat breads.

Calories: 308   Fat (of which saturated fat): 16 g (3 g)   Carbohydrate (of which sugar): 36 g (1 g)   Salt: 1.3 g

vegetable tempura

ginger tofu dip

9 ounces soft silken tofu, drained

¾-inch piece ginger, chopped

1 small shallot, chopped

1 garlic clove, crushed

1 tablespoon wheat- and gluten-free soy sauce

2 teaspoons rice vinegar

batter

1¼ cups gluten-free flour blend

1 egg

1 cup iced water

sunflower oil, for deep-frying

1¼ pounds vegetables, such as asparagus tips, baby carrots, snow peas, baby corn, mushrooms, and broccoli florets

salt and pepper

For the dip, place all the ingredients in a food processor, or use a handheld blender, and process until smooth.

For the batter, beat together the flour, egg, water, and salt and pepper to make a smooth, bubbly batter.

Heat a deep saucepan of oil to 350°F, or until a small cube of bread browns in 30 seconds. Dip the vegetables quickly into the batter, then deep-fry in batches for 1–2 minutes, until they are crisp and rise to the surface. Drain on paper towels and keep hot.

Serve the vegetables immediately with the dip.

Calories: 356   Fat (of which saturated fat): 17.5 g (2.5 g)   Carbohydrate (of which sugar): 34 g (5 g)   Salt: 1 g

spicy falafels

serves 4

1⅔ cups rinsed and drained canned chickpeas (garbanzo beans)

1 small red onion, chopped

2 garlic cloves, crushed

2 teaspoons ground coriander

1½ teaspoons ground cumin

1 teaspoon ground star anise

1 red chile, chopped

1 egg white

½ teaspoon gluten-free baking powder

chickpea (besan) flour, for shaping

sunflower oil, for deep-frying

salt and pepper

salad

1 large orange

2 tablespoons extra virgin olive oil

3 cups arugula leaves

Place the chickpeas, onion, garlic, coriander, cumin, anise, chile, egg white, and salt and pepper in a food processor and process to a firm paste that still has some texture. Stir in the baking powder.

Use a little chickpea flour on your hands to shape the batter into about 12 small balls.

To make the salad, cut all the peel and white pith from the orange and lift out the segments, catching the juice. Whisk the juice with the olive oil and season to taste. Lightly toss the orange segments and arugula with the dressing.

Heat a 1-inch depth of oil in a large saucepan to 350°F, or until a cube of bread browns in 30 seconds. Cook the falafels for about 2 minutes, turning, until golden brown.

Drain the falafels on paper towels and serve with the salad.

Calories: 300   Fat (of which saturated fat): 24 g (3 g)   Carbohydrate (of which sugar): 15 g (5.5 g)   Salt: 0.5 g

gnocchi

serves 4

4 mealy potatoes, such as russets or Yukon Gold

3 tablespoons finely chopped basil

½ teaspoon ground nutmeg

¾ cup gluten-free and wheat-free flour blend, plus extra for dusting

1 medium egg, beaten

4 plum tomatoes, halved

1 red onion, halved

2 garlic cloves

oil, for brushing

salt and pepper

basil leaves, to garnish

Peel the potatoes and cut into chunks. Cook in lightly salted, boiling water for 15–20 minutes, or until tender. Drain thoroughly.

Preheat a broiler to hot. Press the potatoes through a potato ricer or coarse strainer. Add the chopped basil and season well with the nutmeg and salt and pepper. Lightly stir in the flour and add enough egg to make a soft, but not sticky, dough.

Divide the dough into four and roll each piece to a sausage about 8 inches long by 1 inch wide. Cut each into eight to nine slices. Roll each into a ball and press over a floured fork with your thumb, making ridges on one side and an indentation on the other.

Place the tomatoes and onion cut side down onto a baking sheet with the garlic cloves and brush with oil. Cook in the preheated broiler for 8–10 minutes, until the skins are charred. Remove the skins and coarsely chop.

Bring a large saucepan of water to a boil and cook the gnocchi in batches for 4–6 minutes, or until they rise to the surface. Lift out with a slotted spoon.

Serve the gnocchi hot, with the tomato sauce spooned over and garnished with basil leaves.

Calories: 240   Fat (of which saturated fat): 4 g (0.8 g)   Carbohydrate (of which sugar): 45 g (5 g)   Salt: 0.3 g

zucchini quiche

serves 4

dough

1¾ cups gluten- and wheat-free flour blend

½ cup dairy-free soy spread

¼ cup snipped chives

pinch of salt

¼–½ cup cold water

filling

2 tablespoons olive oil

1 small red onion, cut into wedges

2 zucchini, cut into ¾-inch chunks

8 cherry tomatoes, halved

1 extra-large egg, beaten

¾ cup unsweetened dairy-free soy milk

salt and pepper

For the dough, place the flour, spread, chives, and salt in a food processor and process to fine crumbs. Mix in just enough water to bind the mixture to form a firm dough.

Roll out the dough on a lightly floured surface to line a 9-inch loose-bottom tart pan. Prick the bottom with a fork and chill in the refrigerator for 10 minutes.

Preheat the oven to 400°F and preheat a baking sheet. To prevent the pastry shell from becoming soggy, line it with parchment paper and pie weights or dried beans and bake in the preheated oven for 10 minutes. Remove the paper and weights and bake for an additional 5 minutes. Reduce the oven temperature to 375°F.

For the filling, heat the oil in a saucepan and cook the onion and zucchini, stirring often, for 4–5 minutes, or until softened and lightly brown. Invert into the pastry shell with the tomatoes.

Beat the egg with the milk and season well. Pour into the pastry shell. Bake in the preheated oven for 35–40 minutes, or until golden brown and set. Cool for 10 minutes before turning out. Serve the quiche warm or cold.

Calories: 464   Fat (of which saturated fat): 30 g (6 g)   Carbohydrate (of which sugar): 41 g (3 g)   Salt: 0.9 g

3

Main Meals

mushroom pasta

serves 4

10½ ounces dried gluten-free penne (about 3½ cups) or pasta shape of your choice

2 tablespoons olive oil

3½ cups sliced white mushrooms

1 teaspoon dried oregano

1 cup gluten-free vegetable stock

1 tablespoon lemon juice

⅔ cup vegan cream cheese

7 ounces frozen spinach leaves, thawed (about 1¼ cups)

salt and pepper

Cook the pasta in a large saucepan of lightly salted boiling water according to the package directions. Drain, reserving ¾ cup of the cooking liquid.

Meanwhile, heat the oil in a large, heavy skillet over medium heat, add the mushrooms, and cook, stirring frequently, for 8 minutes, or until almost crisp. Stir in the oregano, stock, and lemon juice and cook for 10–12 minutes, or until the sauce is reduced by half.

Stir in the cream cheese and spinach and cook over medium–low heat for 3–5 minutes. Add the reserved cooking liquid, then the cooked pasta. Stir well, season to taste with salt and pepper, and heat through before serving.

| Calories: 400 | Fat (of which saturated fat): 14 g (3 g) | Carbohydrate (of which sugar): 59 g (4 g) | Salt: 0.4 g |

seafood tart

serves 6

14 ounces undyed smoked
haddock, cod, or other
white fish fillet, rinsed
and dried

1¼ cups dairy-free milk

5½ ounces cooked peeled
shrimp

1 cup vegan
cream cheese

3 eggs, beaten

3 tablespoons snipped
fresh chives

pepper

pie dough

1½ cups plus 1 tablespoon
gluten-free white flour

large pinch of salt

⅓ cup plus 1 tablespoon
dairy-free spread, diced,
plus extra for greasing

1 egg yolk

3 tablespoons
ice-cold water

Preheat the oven to 400°F. Lightly grease a 10-inch tart pan.

To make the dough, sift the flour and salt into a mixing bowl, then rub in the spread with your fingertips until the mixture resembles coarse bread crumbs. Stir in the egg yolk, followed by the water, then bring the dough together into a ball. Turn out onto a lightly floured surface and knead until smooth. Wrap in plastic wrap and chill in the refrigerator for 30 minutes.

Meanwhile, put the fish into a shallow saucepan with the milk. Heat gently until simmering, then simmer for 10 minutes, or until just cooked and opaque. Remove the fish with a slotted spoon, let cool a little, then peel away the skin and discard any bones. Flake the fish into large chunks and set aside. Reserve ½ cup of the cooking liquid.

Roll out the dough and use to line the prepared tart pan. To prevent the pastry shell from becoming soggy, line it with parchment paper, fill with pie weights or dried beans, and bake in the preheated oven for 8 minutes. Remove the paper and weights and bake for an additional 5 minutes.

Arrange the fish and shrimp in the pastry shell. Beat together the cream cheese, reserved cooking liquid, eggs, chives, and pepper to taste in a bowl, then pour over the seafood. Bake for 30 minutes, or until the filling is set and golden brown.

Calories: 533   Fat (of which saturated fat): 36 g (14 g)   Carbohydrate (of which sugar): 25 g (0.5 g)   Salt: 2.6 g

baked cod

serves 4

4 thick cod, flounder, or pollock fillets

olive oil, for brushing

8 thin lemon slices

salt and pepper

herb sauce

¼ cup olive oil

1 garlic clove, crushed

¼ cup chopped fresh parsley

2 tablespoons chopped fresh mint

juice of ½ lemon

salt and pepper

Preheat the oven to 400°F. Rinse each fish fillet and pat dry with paper towel, then brush with oil. Place each fillet on a piece of parchment paper that is large enough to encase the fish in a package. Top each fillet with 2 lemon slices and season to taste with salt and pepper. Fold over the parchment paper to encase the fish and bake in the preheated oven for 20 minutes, or until just cooked and opaque.

Meanwhile, to make the herb sauce, put all the ingredients into a food processor and process until finely chopped. Season to taste with salt and pepper.

Carefully unfold each package and place on serving plates. Pour a spoonful of herb sauce over each piece of fish before serving.

Calories: 232   Fat (of which saturated fat): 13.5 g (2 g)   Carbohydrate (of which sugar): 0 g (0 g)   Salt: 0.23 g

shrimp noodles

serves 4

2 tablespoons vegetable oil

1 small red bell pepper, seeded and diced

7 ounces bok choy, stems thinly sliced and leaves left whole

2 large garlic cloves, chopped

1 teaspoon ground turmeric

2 teaspoons garam masala

1 teaspoon chili powder (optional)

½ cup hot gluten-free vegetable stock

2 tablespoons smooth peanut butter

1½ cups coconut milk

1 tablespoon wheat- and gluten-free soy sauce

9 ounces thick rice noodles

10 ounces cooked, peeled large shrimp

Heat the oil in a wok or large, heavy skillet over high heat. Add the red bell pepper, bok choy stems, and garlic and stir-fry for 3 minutes. Add the turmeric, garam masala, chili powder, if using, and bok choy leaves and stir-fry for an additional minute.

Mix the hot stock and peanut butter together in a heatproof bowl until the peanut butter has dissolved, then add to the stir-fry with the coconut milk and soy sauce. Cook for 5 minutes over medium heat, or until reduced and thickened.

Meanwhile, immerse the noodles in a bowl of just boiled water. Let stand for 4 minutes, then drain and refresh the noodles under cold running water. Add the cooked noodles and shrimp to the coconut curry and cook for an additional 2–3 minutes, stirring frequently, until heated through.

Transfer to bowls and serve.

Calories: 564   Fat (of which saturated fat): 26 g (15 g)   Carbohydrate (of which sugar): 55 g (3 g)   Salt: 1.9 g

salmon sticks

serves 3

1 cup fine cornmeal or polenta

1 teaspoon paprika

14 ounces salmon fillet, skinned and sliced into 12 chunky sticks

1 egg, beaten

sunflower oil, for frying

potato wedges

4 mealy potatoes, such as Bintje potatoes or russets, scrubbed and cut into thick wedges

1–2 tablespoons olive oil

½ teaspoon paprika

salt

Preheat the oven to 400°F. To make the wedges, dry the potato wedges on a clean dish towel. Spoon the oil into a roasting pan and put into the preheated oven briefly to heat. Toss the potatoes in the warm oil until well coated. Sprinkle to taste with paprika and salt and roast for 30 minutes, turning halfway through, until crisp and golden.

Meanwhile, mix the cornmeal and paprika together on a plate. Dip each salmon stick into the beaten egg, then roll in the cornmeal mixture until evenly coated.

Heat enough oil to cover the bottom of a large, heavy skillet over medium heat. Carefully arrange half of the salmon sticks in the skillet and cook for 6 minutes, turning halfway through, until golden. Drain on paper towels and keep warm while you cook the remaining sticks. Serve with the potato wedges.

Calories: 677   Fat (of which saturated fat): 30 g (4.5 g)   Carbohydrate (of which sugar): 61 g (1 g)   Salt: 0.25 g

beef stew

serves 4

1 cup plus 1 tablespoon gluten-free white flour, plus extra for flouring

1¾ pounds chuck short ribs or center cut beef shanks, cubed

3 tablespoons olive oil

12 shallots, halved

2 carrots, cut into sticks

1 parsnip, sliced

2 bay leaves

1 tablespoon fresh rosemary

2 cups hard cider

1 cup gluten-free beef stock

1 tablespoon wheat- and gluten-free soy sauce

18 canned chestnuts (about 7 ounces)

1 teaspoon gluten-free baking powder

¼ cup gluten-free vegetable shortening

2 tablespoons fresh thyme

salt and pepper

Preheat the oven to 325°F. Put 3 tablespoons of the flour into a clean plastic bag or on a plate and season generously with salt and pepper. Toss the beef in the seasoned flour until coated. Heat 1 tablespoon of the oil in a large, flameproof casserole dish over medium–high heat. Add one-third of the beef and cook for 5–6 minutes, turning occasionally, until browned all over; the meat may stick to the casserole dish until it is properly sealed. Remove the beef with a slotted spoon. Cook the remaining two batches, adding another tablespoon of oil as necessary. Set aside when all the beef has been sealed. Add the remaining oil to the casserole dish with the shallots, carrots, parsnip, bay leaves, and rosemary and cook for 3 minutes, stirring occasionally. Pour in the cider and beef stock and bring to a boil. Cook over high heat until the alcohol has evaporated and the liquid is reduced. Add the soy, then cook for another 3 minutes. Stir in the chestnuts and beef, cover, and cook in the preheated oven for 1 hour 35 minutes.

Meanwhile, to make the dumplings, combine the remaining flour, baking powder, pinch of salt, shortening, and thyme in a bowl and season to taste with pepper. Mix in enough water to make a soft dough. Divide the dough into walnut-size pieces and, using floured hands, roll each piece into a ball. Add to the casserole dish, cover, and cook for an additional 25 minutes, or until the dumplings are cooked, the stock has formed a thick, rich gravy, and the meat is tender. Season to taste with salt and pepper before serving.

Calories: 709   Fat (of which saturated fat): 32 g (12 g)   Carbohydrate (of which sugar): 47 g (13.5 g)   Salt: 2 g

meatball pasta

serves 4

10½ ounces dried
gluten-free spaghetti

salt and pepper

meatballs

1 cup fresh gluten-free
bread crumbs

1 pound fresh lean
ground beef

1 onion, grated

1 large garlic clove, crushed

1 egg, beaten

salt and pepper

tomato sauce

1 tablespoon olive oil

2 garlic cloves, chopped

2 teaspoons dried oregano

1¼ cups dry white wine

2½ cups tomato puree

1 bay leaf

2 teaspoons tomato paste

½ teaspoon sugar

To make the meatballs, put the bread crumbs, beef, onion, garlic, and egg into a bowl and mix well until combined. Season to taste with salt and pepper, cover, and chill in the refrigerator for 30 minutes.

Meanwhile, make the tomato sauce. Heat the oil in a large, heavy skillet over medium heat and sauté the garlic, stirring, for 1 minute. Add the oregano and cook, stirring, for an additional minute. Pour in the wine and cook over high heat until it has almost evaporated.

Add the tomato puree, bay leaf, tomato paste, and sugar, then stir well. Partly cover the skillet and cook over medium–low heat for 5 minutes.

Form the meatball mixture into walnut-size balls. Add to the sauce, partly cover, and cook for 15–20 minutes, or until the meatballs are cooked through.

Meanwhile, cook the spaghetti in a large saucepan of lightly salted boiling water according to the package directions. Drain, reserving 3 tablespoons of the cooking liquid. Stir the cooking liquid into the sauce before serving with the pasta.

Calories: 640   Fat (of which saturated fat): 17 g (5.9 g)   Carbohydrate (of which sugar): 70 g (5 g)   Salt: 0.5 g

lamb skewers

serves 4

9 ounces fresh lean ground lamb, turkey, or beef

1 onion, finely chopped

1 tablespoon chopped fresh cilantro

1 tablespoon chopped fresh parsley

½ teaspoon ground coriander

¼ teaspoon chili powder

oil, for brushing

salt and pepper

chickpea mash

1 tablespoon olive oil

2 garlic cloves, chopped

1⅔ cups rinsed and drained canned chickpeas (garbanzo beans)

¼ cup dairy-free milk

2 tablespoons chopped fresh cilantro

salt and pepper

cilantro sprigs, to garnish

Soak 12 wooden skewers in water for 30 minutes to prevent them from burning. Meanwhile, put the meat, onion, herbs, spices, and salt and pepper to taste in a food processor. Process until thoroughly combined.

Divide the mixture into 12 portions and, using wet hands, shape each portion into a sausage shape around a skewer. Cover and chill the skewers in the refrigerator for 30 minutes. To cook, preheat a ridged grill pan over medium heat and brush with a little oil. Cook the skewers in two batches, turning occasionally, for 10 minutes, or until browned on all sides and cooked through.

To make the chickpea mash, heat the oil in a saucepan and gently cook the garlic for 2 minutes. Add the chickpeas and milk and heat for a few minutes. Transfer to a food processor or blender and process until smooth. Season to taste with salt and pepper, then stir in the fresh cilantro. Garnish with cilantro sprigs and serve with the skewers.

Calories: 222   Fat (of which saturated fat): 12 g (4 g)   Carbohydrate (of which sugar): 11 g (1.5 g)   Salt: 0.5 g

pork pot pies

serves 4

2 tablespoons sunflower oil

6 shallots, cut into wedges

1¼ pounds diced lean pork

8 ounces cremini mushrooms, quartered

⅔ cup apple juice

1 tablespoon chopped tarragon

salt and pepper

dough

3 potatoes (14 ounces), cut into even chunks

⅓ cup dairy-free olive spread

2 teaspoons chopped tarragon

¾ cup rice flour

1 teaspoon gluten-free baking powder

beaten egg, to glaze

salt and pepper

Preheat the oven to 400°F. Heat the oil in a large saucepan and cook the shallots for 2–3 minutes, stirring occasionally.

Add the pork and cook for 6–8 minutes, stirring, until browned. Add the mushrooms and cook for 2 minutes to soften.

Stir in the apple juice, tarragon, and seasoning. Divide the mixture among four 1¼-cup baking dishes.

To make the dough, cook the potatoes in lightly salted, boiling water until tender. Drain thoroughly and cool, uncovered.

Mash the potatoes, then stir in the spread, tarragon, and salt and pepper. Sift over the rice flour and baking powder and stir in lightly and evenly to make a soft dough, pressing together with your hands.

Divide the dough into four and roll out each to cover the pie dishes, pinching the edges to seal.

Place the pies on a baking sheet, brush the tops with egg, and bake for 35–40 minutes, until golden. Serve hot.

Calories: 608   Fat (of which saturated fat): 30 g (6.5 g)   Carbohydrate (of which sugar): 44.5 g (5.5 g)   Salt: 0.9 g

chicken curry

serves 4

2 tablespoons vegetable oil

4 skinless, boneless chicken breasts (about 1¾ pounds in total), cut into 1-inch pieces

1½ teaspoons cumin seeds

1 large onion, grated

2 fresh green chiles, finely chopped

2 large garlic cloves, grated

1 tablespoon grated fresh ginger

1 teaspoon ground turmeric

1 teaspoon ground coriander

1 teaspoon garam masala

1¼ cups coconut milk

1 cup canned chopped tomatoes

2 teaspoons lemon juice

salt

2 tablespoons chopped fresh cilantro, to garnish

cooked basmati rice, to serve

Heat the oil in a large, heavy saucepan over medium heat. Add the chicken and cook for 5–8 minutes, turning frequently, until lightly brown and cooked through. Remove from the saucepan and set aside. Add the cumin seeds and cook until they begin to darken and sizzle. Stir in the onion, partly cover, and cook over medium–low heat, stirring frequently, for 10 minutes, or until soft and golden. Add the chiles, garlic, ginger, turmeric, ground coriander, and garam masala and cook for 1 minute.

Return the chicken to the saucepan and stir in the coconut milk and tomatoes. Partly cover and cook over medium heat for 15 minutes, until the sauce has reduced and thickened. Stir in the lemon juice and season to taste with salt.

Serve the curry with the basmati rice, sprinkled with fresh cilantro.

Calories: 424   Fat (of which saturated fat): 21 g (12.5 g)   Carbohydrate (of which sugar): 8.5 g (4 g)   Salt: 0.4 g

roasted chicken

serves 4

4 skinless, boneless chicken breasts (about 1¾ pounds in total)

1 tablespoon olive oil

pesto

¾ cup chopped, drained sun-dried tomatoes in oil

2 garlic cloves, crushed

⅓ cup pine nuts, lightly toasted

⅔ cup extra virgin olive oil

Preheat the oven to 400°F. To make the red pesto, put the sun-dried tomatoes, garlic, ¼ cup of the pine nuts, and the oil into a food processor and process to a coarse paste.

Arrange the chicken in a large casserole dish or roasting pan. Brush each breast with the oil, then place a tablespoon of pesto over each breast. Using the back of a spoon, spread the pesto so that it covers the top of each breast. (This pesto recipe makes more than just the ¼ cup used here. Store the extra pesto in an airtight container in the refrigerator for up to one week.)

Roast the chicken in the preheated oven for 30 minutes, or until tender and the juices run clear when a skewer is inserted into the thickest part of the meat.

Serve sprinkled with the remaining toasted pine nuts.

Calories: 690   Fat (of which saturated fat): 51 g (6 g)   Carbohydrate (of which sugar): 5 g (4 g)   Salt: 0.8 g

risotto

serves 4

1¼ pounds butternut squash or acorn squash, peeled and cut into bite-size pieces (about 4 cups)

¼ cup olive oil

1 teaspoon honey

1 cup fresh basil

¼ cup fresh oregano leaves

1 tablespoon dairy-free spread

2 onions, finely chopped

2⅓ cups Arborio risotto rice

¾ cup dry white wine

5 cups gluten-free vegetable stock

salt and pepper

Preheat the oven to 400°F. Put the squash into a roasting pan. Mix 1 tablespoon of the oil with the honey and spoon over the squash. Turn the squash to coat it in the mixture. Roast in the preheated oven for 30–35 minutes, or until tender.

Meanwhile, put the basil and oregano into a food processor with 2 tablespoons of the remaining oil and process until finely chopped and blended. Set aside.

Heat the spread and remaining oil in a large, heavy saucepan over medium heat. Add the onions and cook, stirring occasionally, for 8 minutes, or until soft and golden. Add the rice and cook for 2 minutes, stirring to coat the grains in the oil mixture.

Pour in the wine and bring to a boil. Reduce the heat slightly and cook until the wine is almost absorbed. Add the stock, a little at a time, and cook over medium–low heat, stirring constantly, for 20 minutes.

Gently stir in the herb oil and squash until thoroughly mixed into the rice and cook for an additional 5 minutes, or until the rice is creamy and cooked but retaining a little bite in the center of the grain. Season with salt and pepper before serving.

Calories: 652   Fat (of which saturated fat): 15.5 g (2.5 g)   Carbohydrate (of which sugar): 108 g (11 g)   Salt: 0.5 g

tofu cakes

makes 8

12 ounces firm tofu, drained and coarsely grated

1 lemongrass stem, outer layer discarded, finely chopped

2 garlic cloves, chopped

1-inch piece fresh ginger, grated

2 kaffir lime leaves, finely chopped (optional)

2 shallots, finely chopped

2 fresh red chiles, seeded and finely chopped

¼ cup chopped fresh cilantro

¾ cup gluten-free white flour, plus extra for flouring

½ teaspoon salt

sunflower oil, for frying

gluten-free sweet chili dipping sauce, to serve

Mix the tofu with the lemongrass, garlic, ginger, lime leaves, if using, shallots, chiles, and cilantro in a mixing bowl. Stir in the flour and salt to make a coarse, sticky paste. Cover and chill in the refrigerator for 1 hour to let the mixture become slightly firm.

Form the mixture into large walnut-size balls and, using floured hands, flatten into patties until you have eight cakes. Heat enough oil to cover the bottom of a large, heavy skillet over medium heat. Cook the cakes in two batches, turning halfway through, for 4–6 minutes, or until golden brown. Drain on paper towels and serve warm with the chili dip.

Calories: 103   Fat (of which saturated fat): 5 g (0.7 g)   Carbohydrate (of which sugar): 10 g (0.3 g)   Salt: 0.3 g

eggplant stew

serves 4

1 eggplant, cubed

3 tablespoons olive oil

1 large onion, thinly sliced

1 carrot, diced

2 garlic cloves, chopped

1⅔ cups sliced white mushrooms

2 teaspoons ground coriander

2 teaspoons cumin seeds

1 teaspoon chili powder

1 teaspoon ground turmeric

2½ cups canned chopped tomatoes

1¼ cups gluten-free vegetable stock

½ cup chopped plumped dried apricots

1⅔ cups rinsed and drained canned chickpeas (garbanzo beans)

5 cups hot gluten-free vegetable stock

1¼ cups instant polenta

2 tablespoons cilantro, to garnish

Preheat the broiler to medium. Toss the eggplant in 1 tablespoon of the oil and arrange in the broiler pan. Cook under the preheated broiler for 20 minutes, turning occasionally, until softened and beginning to blacken around the edges—brush with more oil if the eggplant becomes too dry.

Heat the remaining oil in a large, heavy saucepan over medium heat. Add the onion and cook, stirring occasionally, for 8 minutes, or until soft and golden. Add the carrot, garlic, and mushrooms and cook for 5 minutes. Add the spices and cook, stirring continuously, for an additional minute.

Add the tomatoes and stock, stir well, and bring to a boil. Reduce the heat and simmer for 10 minutes, or until the sauce begins to thicken and reduce.

Add the eggplant, apricots, and chickpeas, partly cover and cook for an additional 10 minutes, stirring occasionally.

Meanwhile, to make the polenta, pour the hot stock into a nonstick saucepan and bring to a boil. Pour in the polenta in a steady stream, stirring continuously with a wooden spoon. Reduce the heat to low and cook for 1–2 minutes, or until the polenta thickens to a mashed potato-like consistency. Serve the stew with the polenta, sprinkled with the fresh cilantro.

Calories: 440   Fat (of which saturated fat): 12 g (1.5 g)   Carbohydrate (of which sugar): 65 g (16 g)   Salt: 0.2 g

spice-crusted fish

serves 4

4 large or 8 small sea bass
fillets (about 1½ pounds
in total weight)

1 egg white

2 tablespoons sunflower
oil, for frying

mixed salad greens,
to serve

spice crust

1½ tablespoons coriander
seeds

1 tablespoon cumin seeds

2 teaspoons fennel seeds

1 teaspoon black
peppercorns

½ teaspoon salt

cucumber sauce

3-inch piece cucumber

½ cup plain soy yogurt

2 tablespoons chopped
fresh mint

salt and pepper

To make the spice crust, crush the coriander, cumin, fennel,
peppercorns, and salt in a mortar and pestle or spice mill.
Transfer to a wide dish and mix evenly.

Brush the fish fillets with egg white, then press into the
spice mixture to coat evenly. Cover and let marinate in the
refrigerator for about 30 minutes.

Meanwhile, to make the cucumber sauce, coarsely grate the
cucumber and sprinkle lightly with salt. Let stand for 10
minutes, then rinse and dry. Stir into the yogurt and add the
mint with seasoning to taste.

Heat the oil in a wide, heavy skillet and cook the fish over high
heat for 4–6 minutes, depending on thickness, turning once,
until golden and just cooked through.

Drain the fish on paper towels and serve immediately with the
cucumber sauce and mixed salad greens.

Calories: 229   Fat (of which saturated fat): 12 g (1.5 g)   Carbohydrate (of which sugar): 1 g (1 g)   Salt: 0.9 g

potato tortilla

serves 4

3 white round or red-skinned potatoes, cut into bite-size cubes

1 tablespoon olive oil

1 tablespoon dairy-free spread

1 onion, thinly sliced

6 eggs, lightly beaten

salt and pepper

Preheat the broiler to medium. Cook the potatoes in a saucepan of salted boiling water for 10–12 minutes, or until tender. Drain well and set aside.

Meanwhile, heat the oil and spread in a medium skillet with a heatproof handle over medium heat. (If the handle is not heatproof, wrap with a double layer of aluminum foil.) Add the onion and cook, stirring occasionally, for 8 minutes, or until soft and golden. Add the potatoes and cook for an additional 5 minutes, stirring to prevent them from sticking. Spread the onions and potatoes evenly over the bottom of the skillet. Season the eggs with salt and pepper and pour over the onion and potatoes. Cook for 5–6 minutes, or until the eggs are just set and the bottom of the tortilla is lightly golden.

Place the skillet under the preheated broiler and cook the top of the tortilla for 2–3 minutes, until it is just set and risen. Cut into wedges to serve.

Calories: 258   Fat (of which saturated fat): 16 g (4 g)   Carbohydrate (of which sugar): 17 g (2 g)   Salt: 0.4 g

vegetable curry

3 carrots

3 white round potatoes

2 tablespoons vegetable oil

1½ teaspoons cumin seeds

seeds from 5 green cardamom pods

1½ teaspoons mustard seeds

2 onions, grated

1 teaspoon ground turmeric

1 teaspoon ground coriander

1 bay leaf

1½ teaspoons chili powder

1 tablespoon grated fresh ginger

2 garlic cloves, crushed

1 cup tomato puree

1 cup gluten-free vegetable stock

¾ cup frozen peas

4 ounces frozen spinach, thawed (about ¾ cup)

salt

8 wheat- and gluten-free pancakes

Put the carrots and potatoes into a steamer and steam until just tender but retaining some bite.

Heat the oil in a large, heavy saucepan over medium heat and add the cumin seeds, cardamom seeds, and mustard seeds. When they begin to darken and sizzle, add the onions, partly cover, and cook over medium–low heat, stirring frequently, for 10 minutes.

Add the other spices, ginger, and garlic and cook, stirring continuously, for 1 minute. Add the tomato puree, stock, potatoes, and carrots, partly cover, and cook for 10–15 minutes, or until the vegetables are tender. Add the peas and spinach, then cook for an additional 2–3 minutes. Season to taste with salt before serving with the pancakes.

Calories: 418   Fat (of which saturated fat): 15 g (2 g)   Carbohydrate (of which sugar): 56 g (9 g)   Salt: 1.8 g

pesto hash browns

serves 4

2 pounds Binjte potatoes

sunflower oil, for frying

2 tablespoons vegan pesto

1 tablespoon boiling water

1 tablespoon extra virgin
olive oil

salt

roasted vegetables

2 tablespoons extra virgin
olive oil

1 tablespoon balsamic
vinegar

1 teaspoon honey

1 red bell pepper, seeded
and quartered

2 zucchini, sliced

2 red onions, quartered

1 small fennel bulb,
cut into thin wedges

16 vine-ripened tomatoes

8 garlic cloves

2 fresh rosemary sprigs

For the roasted vegetables, mix the oil, vinegar, and honey together in a large, shallow dish. Add the red bell pepper, zucchini, onions, fennel, tomatoes, garlic, and rosemary to the dish and toss in the marinade. Let marinate for at least 1 hour.

Preheat the oven to 400°F. Meanwhile, to make hash browns, cook the potatoes in a saucepan of lightly salted boiling water for 8–10 minutes, until partly cooked. Let cool, then coarsely grate.

Transfer the vegetables, except the tomatoes and garlic, and the marinade to a roasting pan. Roast in the preheated oven for 25 minutes, then add the tomatoes and garlic and roast for an additional 15 minutes, or until the vegetables are tender and slightly blackened around the edges.

Meanwhile, cook the hash browns. Take one-quarter of the grated potato in your hands and form into a roughly shaped patty. Heat just enough oil to cover the bottom of a skillet over medium heat. Put the patties, two at a time, into the skillet and flatten with a spatula to form circles about 3/4 inch thick. Cook the hash browns for 6 minutes on each side, or until golden brown and crisp.

Mix together the pesto, boiling water, and olive oil to make a pesto dressing. To serve, top each hash brown with the roasted vegetables and drizzle with a little pesto dressing.

Calories: 391   Fat (of which saturated fat): 19 g (2 g)   Carbohydrate (of which sugar): 51 g (11 g)   Salt: 0.1 g

4

Desserts & Baking

coconut macaroons

makes about 26

½ cup skinned pistachio nuts

⅓ cup confectioners' sugar

1 tablespoon rice flour

2 egg whites

¼ cup superfine sugar (or ¼ cup granulated sugar processed in a blender for 1 minute)

¾ cup dry shredded coconut

1 tablespoon chopped mint

pistachios, to decorate

Preheat the oven to 350°F. Line two cookie sheets with parchment paper.

Place the pistachio nuts, confectioners' sugar, and rice flour in a food processor and process until finely ground.

Whisk the egg whites in a clean, dry bowl until stiff, then gradually whisk in the superfine sugar. Fold in the pistachio mixture, coconut, and mint.

Spoon the mixture in small rocky mounds onto the cookie sheets and press a pistachio on top of each.

Bake for about 20 minutes, until firm and just beginning to brown. Cool on the cookie sheets and serve.

Calories: 42   Fat (of which saturated fat): 2.5 g (1.5 g)   Carbohydrate (of which sugar): 4 g (4 g)   Salt: Trace

mocha brownies

makes 12 brownies

⅓ cup plus 1 tablespoon dairy-free spread, plus extra for greasing

5½ ounces good-quality bittersweet chocolate (about 70 percent cocoa solids)

1 teaspoon strong instant coffee

1 teaspoon vanilla extract

1 cup ground almonds

¾ cup plus 2 tablespoons granulated sugar

4 eggs, separated

confectioners' sugar, to decorate (optional)

Preheat the oven to 350°F. Grease an 8-inch square cake pan and line the bottom.

Melt the chocolate and spread in a heatproof bowl placed over a saucepan of gently simmering water, making sure that the bottom of the bowl does not touch the water. Stir occasionally until the chocolate and spread have melted and are smooth.

Carefully remove the bowl from the heat. Let cool slightly, then stir in the coffee and vanilla extract. Add the almonds and sugar and mix well until combined. Lightly beat the egg yolks in a separate bowl, then stir into the chocolate mixture.

Whisk the egg whites in a clean large bowl until they form stiff peaks. Gently fold a large spoonful of the egg whites into the chocolate mixture, then fold in the remainder until completely incorporated.

Spoon the batter into the prepared pan and bake in the preheated oven for 35–40 minutes, or until risen and firm on top but still slightly gooey in the center. Let cool in the pan, then invert onto a plate, remove the parchment paper, and cut into 12 pieces. Dust with confectioners' sugar before serving, if liked.

Calories: 270   Fat (of which saturated fat): 18 g (4.5 g)   Carbohydrate (of which sugar): 22 g (22 g)   Salt: 0.3 g

orange syrup cake

makes 9 slices

dairy-free margarine,
for greasing

6 eggs, separated

1 cup granulated sugar

grated rind of 3 oranges

1½ cups ground almonds

topping

juice of 3 oranges

3 tablespoons honey

Preheat the oven to 350°F. Grease an 8-inch square cake pan and line the bottom. Beat the egg yolks with the sugar, orange rind, and almonds in a large mixing bowl.

Whisk the egg whites in a separate clean large bowl until they form stiff peaks. Fold a spoonful of the egg whites into the almond mixture, then fold in the remainder. Carefully pour the batter into the prepared cake pan.

Bake in the preheated oven for 45–50 minutes, or until a toothpick inserted into the center of the cake comes out clean. Let cool in the pan.

To make the topping, put the orange juice and honey into a small saucepan and bring to a boil, stir once, then cook, without stirring, for 6–8 minutes, or until reduced, thickened, and syrupy. Using a fork, pierce the cake all over, then pour the syrup over the top and let soak in before serving.

Calories: 282   Fat (of which saturated fat): 14 g (2 g)   Carbohydrate (of which sugar): 30 g (30 g)   Salt: 0.2 g

cream puffs

serves 4

¾ cup plus 2 tablespoons gluten- and wheat-free flour blend

½ teaspoon xanthan gum

¼ cup dairy-free sunflower spread, plus extra for greasing

1 cup water

2 eggs, beaten

1 cup tofu-base cream cheese substitute

½ teaspoon vanilla extract

compote

12 ounces mixed berries, such as raspberries, blueberries, and cherries

3 tablespoons granulated sugar

seeds from 1 vanilla bean

Preheat the oven to 425°F. Grease two baking sheets.

Sift together the flour and xanthan gum. Melt the spread with the water and bring to a boil. Remove from the heat and quickly beat in all of the flour mixture. Cool for 1 minute. Gradually beat in the eggs with an electric mixer to make a thick, glossy dough.

Fit a ½-inch plain piping tip in a pastry bag and pipe about 16 golf ball-size balls of dough onto the baking sheets.

Bake in the preheated oven for 20–25 minutes, or until risen and golden brown. Cut a slit in each puffed-up ball to let steam escape and return to the oven for 1 minute. Let cool on a wire rack.

Mix the tofu cheese with the vanilla and pipe into the cooled puffed-up balls.

For the compote, place the fruit, sugar, and vanilla in a saucepan and heat gently until the sugar dissolves and the fruit juice runs. Spoon over the cream puffs to serve.

Calories: 460   Fat (of which saturated fat): 34 g (8 g)   Carbohydrate (of which sugar): 30 g (8 g)   Salt: 1 g

chocolate cake

⅓ cup plus 1 tablespoon dairy-free spread, plus extra for greasing

½ cup granulated sugar

2 eggs, lightly beaten

¾ cup gluten-free all-purpose flour

1 teaspoon gluten-free baking powder

2 tablespoons unsweetened cocoa powder

finely pared strips of orange rind, to decorate

mousse

7 ounces good-quality bittersweet chocolate (about 70 percent cocoa solids)

grated rind of 2 oranges and juice of 1

4 eggs, separated

Preheat the oven to 350°F. Grease a 9-inch round springform cake pan and line the bottom with parchment paper.

Cream the sugar and spread together in a mixing bowl until pale and fluffy. Gradually add the eggs, beating well with a wooden spoon between each addition. Sift the flour, baking powder, and cocoa powder together, fold half into the egg mixture, then fold in the remainder. Spoon the batter into the prepared pan and level the surface with the back of a spoon. Bake in the preheated oven for 20 minutes, until risen and firm to the touch. Let stand in the pan to cool completely.

Meanwhile, melt the chocolate in a heatproof bowl placed over a saucepan of gently simmering water, making sure that the bottom of the bowl does not touch the water. Let cool, then stir in the orange rind and juice and the egg yolks.

Whisk the egg whites in a clean large bowl until they form stiff peaks. Gently fold a large spoonful of the egg whites into the chocolate mixture, then fold in the remainder. Spoon the mixture on top of the cooked, cooled sponge and level the top with the back of a spoon. Alternatively, remove the sponge from the pan, slice through, and sandwich with the mousse. Place in the refrigerator to set. Remove the sides of the pan if not removed earlier (though not the bottom) before decorating with orange rind and serving.

Calories: 407   Fat (of which saturated fat): 24 g (8.5 g)   Carbohydrate (of which sugar): 39 g (29 g)   Salt: 0.7 g

panna cotta

serves 4

4 sheets gelatin

⅓ cup plus 2 tablespoons almond milk

1¾ cups canned coconut milk

1 lemongrass stem, bruised

strip of lime zest

¼ cup plus 1 tablespoon acacia honey

1 small pineapple

1 tablespoon finely grated ginger

½ teaspoon ground cinnamon

juice of 1 lime

dry shredded coconut, toasted, to decorate

Place the gelatin in a wide dish and pour over the almond milk. Let stand for 10 minutes.

Place the coconut milk, lemongrass, and lime zest in a saucepan and heat gently, without boiling, for about 10 minutes. Add the gelatin mixture and ¼ cup of the honey and stir over low heat until thoroughly dissolved.

Strain the mixture into four 1-cup dishes or molds. Let stand in the refrigerator until set.

Peel, core, and thinly slice the pineapple. Sprinkle over the ginger, cinnamon, lime juice, and the remaining honey, turning to coat evenly. Cover and let stand for at least 1 hour.

To serve, quickly dip the molds into hot water and invert onto serving plates. Serve with the spiced pineapple with the juices spooned over. Sprinkle with shreds of coconut to decorate.

Calories: 275   Fat (of which saturated fat): 17.5 g (15 g)   Carbohydrate (of which sugar): 27 g (24 g)   Salt: Trace

apricot cookies

makes about 16

⅓ cup dairy-free sunflower spread, plus extra for greasing

⅓ cup firmly packed light brown sugar

1 egg, beaten

½ teaspoon grated nutmeg

1 teaspoon vanilla extract

1½ cups gluten-free and wheat-free flour blend

2¼ teaspoons gluten-free baking powder

heaping ⅛ teaspoon salt

1⅓ cups coarsely chopped plumped dried apricots

¾ cup coarsely chopped pecans

Preheat the oven to 400°F. Grease two cookie sheets.

Place the spread, sugar, egg, nutmeg, and vanilla in a bowl and beat until smooth. Stir in the flour, baking powder, salt, apricots, and pecans, mixing to form a soft dough.

Use a tablespoon to place mounds of dough on the cookie sheets, pressing with a fork to flatten slightly.

Bake the cookies for 12–15 minutes, or until golden brown. Transfer to a wire rack to cool.

Calories: 165   Fat (of which saturated fat): 9 g (1.5 g)   Carbohydrate (of which sugar): 18.5 g (10 g)   Salt: 0.2 g

strawberry roll

sunflower oil, for greasing

3 extra-large eggs

2/3 cup granulated sugar,
plus extra to sprinkle

1/2 teaspoon almond extract

1/3 cup plus 2 tablespoons
gluten-free cornstarch

3/4 cup ground almonds

confectioners' sugar, to
decorate

filling

1 cup vegan cream cheese

1 tablespoon confectioners'
sugar

1 1/4 cups sliced strawberries

Preheat the oven to 350°F. Grease a 13 x 9-inch jelly roll pan and line with nonstick parchment paper.

Place the eggs, sugar, and almond extract in a large bowl over a saucepan of hot, not boiling, water and whisk for about 10 minutes, until thick enough to hold a trail when the whisk is lifted.

Remove from the heat and whisk in the cornstarch, then fold in the ground almonds lightly and evenly.

Spread the batter into the pan and bake for 12–15 minutes, until just firm and lightly browned.

Place a sheet of nonstick parchment paper on the counter and sprinkle with confectioners' sugar. Invert the pan over the paper to turn out the sponge. Remove the lining paper and trim the edges from the sponge. Cover with a clean dish towel and let cool.

To make the filling, beat together the vegan cream cheese and confectioners' sugar and spread over the sponge. Top with sliced strawberries and carefully roll up from one short edge.

Place on a serving plate with the seam underneath, and sprinkle with confectioners' sugar to serve.

Calories: 371   Fat (of which saturated fat): 21.5 g (4 g)   Carbohydrate (of which sugar): 37 g (29 g)   Salt: 0.5 g

banana muffins

makes 12

1 cup plus 3 tablespoons gluten-free all-purpose flour

1 teaspoon gluten-free baking powder

pinch of salt

¾ cup granulated sugar

⅓ cup plus 2 teaspoons dairy-free milk

2 eggs, lightly beaten

⅔ cup dairy-free spread, melted

2 small bananas, mashed

frosting

¼ cup vegan cream cheese

2 tablespoons dairy-free spread

¼ teaspoon ground cinnamon

¾ cup confectioners' sugar

Preheat the oven to 400°F. Place 12 baking cups in a muffin pan. Sift the flour, baking powder, and salt together into a mixing bowl. Stir in the sugar.

Beat the milk, eggs, and spread together in a separate bowl until combined. Slowly stir into the flour mixture without beating. Fold in the mashed bananas.

Spoon the mixture into the baking cups and bake in the preheated oven for 20 minutes, until risen and golden. Invert onto a wire rack and let cool.

To make the frosting, beat the cream cheese and spread together in a bowl, then beat in the cinnamon and confectioners' sugar until smooth and creamy. Chill the frosting in the refrigerator for about 15 minutes, until firm, then top each muffin with a spoonful.

Calories: 287   Fat (of which saturated fat): 16 g (4.5 g)   Carbohydrate (of which sugar): 33 g (24 g)   Salt: 0.7 g

apple stacks

serves 4
pancakes

⅓ cup dairy-free
sunflower spread, plus
extra for greasing

¼ cup superfine sugar
(or ¼ cup granulated
sugar processed in a
blender for 1 minute)

⅔ cup hazelnuts, toasted
and skinned

¾ cup plus 2 tablespoons
gluten-free and wheat-
free flour blend, plus
extra for dusting

1 egg yolk

caramel apples

3 crisp apples,
such as Macintosh, Gala,
or Cortland

¼ cup sunflower spread

¼ cup demerara sugar
or other raw sugar

chopped toasted hazelnuts,
to decorate

Preheat the oven to 400°F. Grease a large baking sheet.

Place the sunflower spread, sugar, hazelnuts, flour, and egg yolk in a bowl and mix well to bind to a soft dough.

Roll out the dough on a lightly floured surface to about ¼ inch thick and use a 2¾-inch cutter to cut 12 circles. Lift onto the baking sheet and bake for 10–12 minutes, or until golden. Cool for 2 minutes, then finish cooling on a wire rack.

Peel, core, and slice the apples. Melt the spread in a heavy saucepan with the apples and sugar, stirring over high heat until golden brown.

Stack the "pancakes" in threes with apple slices between each layer, spooning over the caramel sauce. Sprinkle with chopped hazelnuts and serve warm.

Calories: 699   Fat (of which saturated fat): 45 g (8 g)   Carbohydrate (of which sugar): 70 g (47 g)   Salt: 0.7 g

mango cheesecake

serves 8

⅓ cup dairy-free spread, plus extra for greasing

1½ cups plain vanilla, cinnamon, or chocolate gluten-free and dairy-free cookie crumbs

¼ cup plus 1 tablespoon ground almonds

filling

1 large mango, pitted, peeled, and diced

juice of 1 lemon

1 cup plain soy yogurt

1 tablespoon gluten-free cornstarch

3 tablespoons maple syrup

2 cups vegan cream cheese

topping

3 tablespoons maple syrup

1 small mango, pitted, peeled, and sliced

Preheat the oven to 350°F. Lightly grease a 9-inch round springform cake pan. To make the cookie crumb crust, melt the spread in a medium saucepan, then stir in the cookie crumbs and almonds. Press the mixture into the bottom of the prepared cake pan to make an even layer. Bake in the preheated oven for 10 minutes.

Meanwhile, to make the filling, put the mango, lemon juice, yogurt, cornstarch, maple syrup, and cream cheese into a food processor or blender and process until smooth and creamy. Pour the mixture over the cookie crumb crust and smooth with the back of a spoon. Bake for 25–30 minutes, or until golden and set. Let cool in the pan, then transfer to a wire rack and chill in the refrigerator for 30 minutes, until firm.

To make the topping, heat the maple syrup in a skillet. Brush the top of the cheesecake with the maple syrup. Add the mango to the remaining maple syrup in the saucepan and cook for 1 minute, stirring. Let cool slightly, then arrange the mango slices on top of the cheesecake. Pour over any remaining syrup before serving.

Calories: 429   Fat (of which saturated fat): 31 g (8 g)   Carbohydrate (of which sugar): 32 g (18 g)   Salt: 1 g

tapioca

serves 6

1 tablespoon dairy-free sunflower spread, plus extra for greasing

1⅓ cups small pearl tapioca

2 cups rice milk

⅓ cup granulated sugar

seeds from 2 cardamom pods, lightly crushed

1 bay leaf

½ teaspoon orange flower water

6 fresh figs

pomegranate syrup, for drizzling

Grease a 7-inch square cake pan. Place the tapioca and rice milk in a saucepan and bring to a boil. Reduce the heat and stir in the sugar, cardamom, bay leaf, and spread.

Cover and cook gently, stirring often, for 20–25 minutes, or until the grains are tender.

Remove the bay leaf, stir in the orange flower water, then spread into the pan and let cool. Chill in the refrigerator until set.

To serve, invert the tapioca and cut into diamond shapes. Quarter the figs and arrange on plates with the tapioca shapes. Drizzle with pomegranate syrup and serve.

Calories: 327   Fat (of which saturated fat): 4 g (0.5 g)   Carbohydrate (of which sugar): 67 g (22 g)   Salt: Trace

pear sorbet

serves 6

⅓ cup granulated sugar

1 tablespoon honey

1 cup water

1–2 just-ripe pears, such as Bosc, peeled, cored, and sliced (about 1⅔ cups)

2 teaspoons finely chopped fresh ginger

3 tablespoons lemon juice

Put the sugar, honey, and water into a saucepan over medium heat and heat, stirring, until the sugar has dissolved. Add the pears and ginger and simmer for 5 minutes, then add the lemon juice.

Transfer the pears and cooking liquid into a food processor or blender and process until almost smooth. Carefully pour the mixture into a freezerproof container with a lid and let cool.

Put in the freezer for 2 hours, until the edges and bottom of the pear mixture are frozen. Remove the container from the freezer and mix with a fork so that the frozen part of the mixture is blended with the unfrozen part. Replace the lid and return to the freezer for an additional 1½ hours.

Repeat the mixing process and freeze for another hour, until the mixture forms ice crystals. Serve at this stage or return to the freezer until required, then remove 30 minutes before serving and mix again with a fork.
Serve spooned into glasses.

Calories: 113   Fat (of which saturated fat): 0.1 g (0 g)   Carbohydrate (of which sugar): 28 g (28 g)   Salt: Trace

apple crisp

serves 4

4 apples, peeled, cored and diced

5 plums, halved, pitted, and quartered

¼ cup fresh apple juice

2 tablespoons firmly packed light brown sugar

topping

¾ cup plus 2 tablespoons gluten-free flour

⅓ cup dairy-free spread, diced

½ cup buckwheat flakes

½ cup rice flakes

3 tablespoons sunflower seeds

¼ cup firmly packed light brown sugar

¼ teaspoon ground cinnamon

Preheat the oven to 350°F. Mix the apples, plums, apple juice, and sugar together in a 9-inch round pie plate.

To make the topping, sift the flour into a mixing bowl and rub in the spread with your fingertips until it resembles coarse bread crumbs. Stir in the buckwheat and rice flakes, sunflower seeds, sugar, and cinnamon, then spoon the topping over the fruit in the dish.

Bake the crisp in the preheated oven for 30–35 minutes, or until the topping is lightly browned and crisp.

| Calories: 484 | Fat (of which saturated fat): 19 g (4 g) | Carbohydrate (of which sugar): 73 g (42 g) | Salt: 0.6 g |

fruit bake

serves 6

1 tablespoon sunflower oil

¾ cup gluten-free and wheat-free flour blend

1⅛ teaspoons gluten-free baking powder

pinch of salt

2 tablespoons vanilla sugar

2 eggs, beaten

1 cup sweetened soy milk

1½ cups raspberries

3 nectarines, halved, pitted, and coarsely chopped

confectioners' sugar, for sprinkling

Preheat the oven to 425°F. Grease a 2-quart shallow metal dutch oven or roasting pan with the oil.

Place the flour, baking powder, salt, sugar, eggs, and milk in a bowl and beat to a smooth, bubbly batter. Add the raspberries.

Place the dutch oven in the oven for 5 minutes, until very hot. Add the nectarines and heat for an additional minute. Remove from the oven and quickly pour in the batter and raspberries.

Bake for 25–30 minutes, until just set, risen, and golden brown. Sprinkle with confectioners' sugar and serve warm.

Calories: 147   Fat (of which saturated fat): 3 g (0.5 g)   Carbohydrate (of which sugar): 26 g (14 g)   Salt: 0.2 g

tomato focaccia

makes 1 loaf (serves 10)

3 tablespoons olive oil, plus extra for brushing

1⅔ cups buckwheat flour

1¾ cups potato flour

1¼ cups rice flour

2 teaspoons xanthan gum

2¼ teaspoons gluten-free fast-action yeast

1½ teaspoon salt

½ teaspoon black onion seeds

20 sun-dried tomato pieces, soaked, drained, and chopped

2½ cups lukewarm water

1 medium egg, beaten

2 garlic cloves, cut into slivers

few sprigs of fresh oregano

Brush a 13 x 9-inch baking pan with oil. Mix the flours, xanthan gum, yeast, salt, and onion seeds in a bowl and stir in the tomatoes.

Make a well in the center and stir in the water, egg, and 1 tablespoon of oil to make a soft dough. Beat the dough firmly, using a wooden spoon, for 4–5 minutes, then spoon in the baking pan, spreading evenly with a spatula.

Cover with oiled plastic wrap and let stand in a warm place for about 1 hour, or until doubled in size. Preheat the oven to 425°F.

Press pieces of garlic and oregano into the dough at intervals. Drizzle with the remaining oil, then bake in the preheated oven for 25–30 minutes, or until firm and golden brown. Invert and cool on a wire rack.

Calories: 229   Fat (of which saturated fat): 7 g (1 g)   Carbohydrate (of which sugar): 39 g (1 g)   Salt: 1 g

pepper cornbread

makes 1 loaf (serves 10)

3 tablespoons olive oil, plus extra for oiling

1 large red bell pepper, seeded and sliced

1¼ cups fine cornmeal or polenta

¾ cup plus 2 tablespoons gluten-free bread flour

1 tablespoon gluten-free baking powder

1 teaspoon salt

2 teaspoons sugar

1 cup plus 2 tablespoons dairy-free milk

2 eggs, lightly beaten

Preheat the oven to 400°F. Lightly oil an 8½-inch loaf pan. Arrange the red bell pepper slices on a baking sheet and roast in the preheated oven for 35 minutes, until tender and the skin begins to blister. Set aside to cool slightly, then peel away the skin.

Meanwhile, mix together the cornmeal, flour, baking powder, salt, and sugar in a large mixing bowl. Beat together the milk, eggs, and oil in a separate bowl or pitcher and gradually add to the flour mixture. Beat with a wooden spoon to make a thick, smooth, batterlike consistency.

Finely chop the red bell pepper and fold into the cornmeal mixture, then spoon into the prepared pan. Bake in the preheated oven for 30 minutes, until lightly golden. Let cool in the pan for 10 minutes, then run a knife around the edge of the pan and invert the loaf onto a wire rack to cool. To keep fresh, wrap the loaf in aluminum foil or seal in a plastic bag.

Calories: 180   Fat (of which saturated fat): 7 g (1.1 g)   Carbohydrate (of which sugar): 23 g (2.5 g)   Salt: 1 g

holiday fruitcake

serves 6

⅓ cup dairy-free sunflower spread, plus extra for greasing

1⅓ cups dried fruit, such as raisins and currants

½ cup apple juice

⅓ cup plus 1 tablespoon gluten- and wheat-free flour blend

1 teaspoon ground allspice

⅔ cup fresh bread crumbs from a gluten-free loaf

⅓ cup firmly packed dark brown sugar

1 apple, cored and grated

2 tablespoons chopped almonds, blanched

finely grated rind 1 lemon

1 egg, beaten

sauce

1 cup vegan cream cheese

finely grated rind ½ orange, plus extra to decorate

1 tablespoon brandy (optional)

Grease six ⅔-cup dariole molds or other individual molds and line the bottom of each with a circle of nonstick parchment paper. Soak the dried fruit in the apple juice for about 1 hour.

Place all the main ingredients in a large bowl and mix thoroughly. Pack firmly into the molds.

Cover the molds with a double layer of aluminum foil, twisting over at the edges to seal. Fill a steamer halfway with water and bring to a boil. Steam the fruitcakes for 50 minutes, or until firm, adding additional water, if necessary.

For the sauce, mix together all the ingredients until smooth. Turn out the fruitcakes and serve with the sauce decorated with orange rind.

If not serving immediately, remove the foil and cool, cover with clean aluminum foil, and store in the refrigerator for up to two weeks. Reheat in a steamer for 15 minutes.

Calories: 410   Fat (of which saturated fat): 23 g (5 g)   Carbohydrate (of which sugar): 48 g (38 g)   Salt: 0.8 g